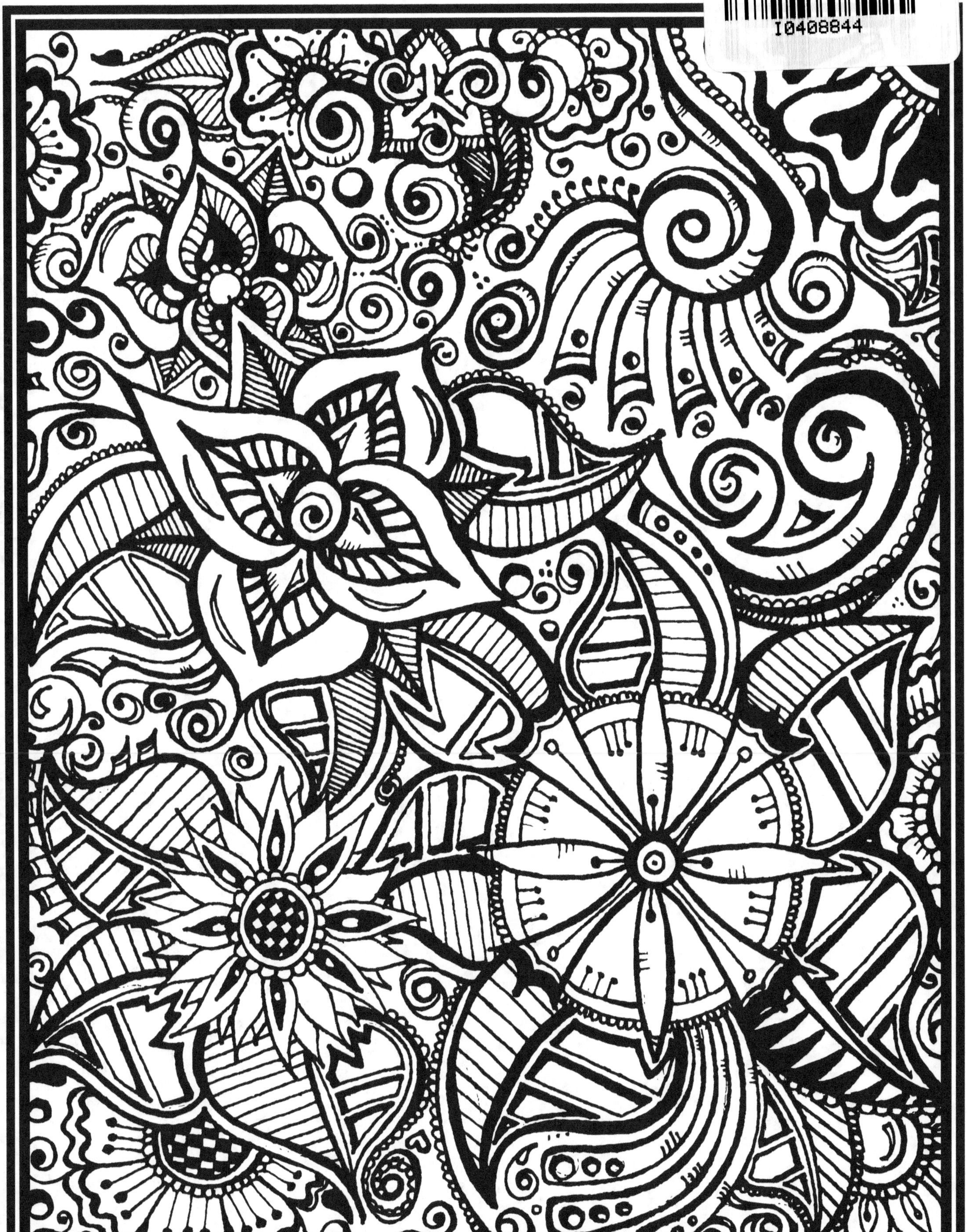

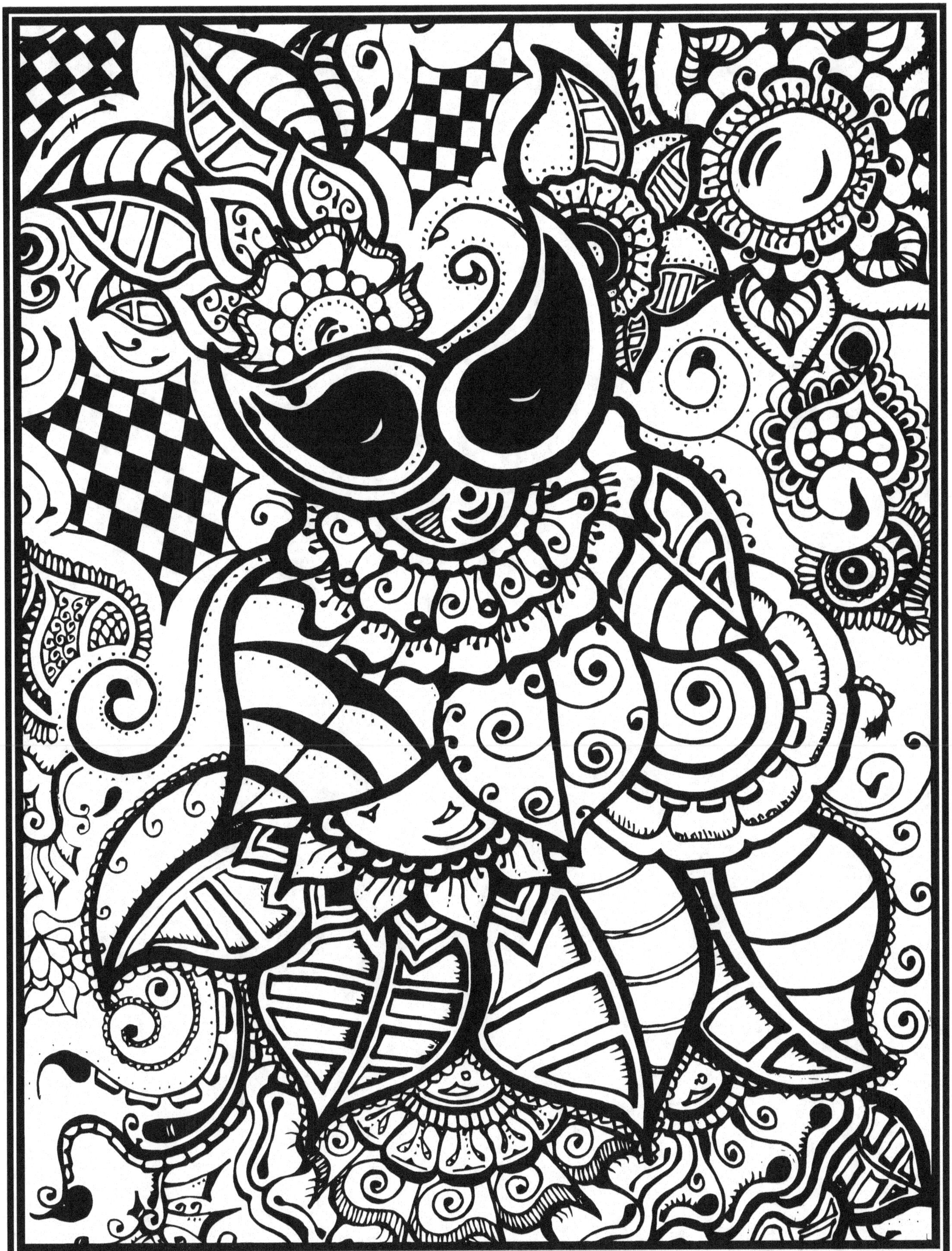

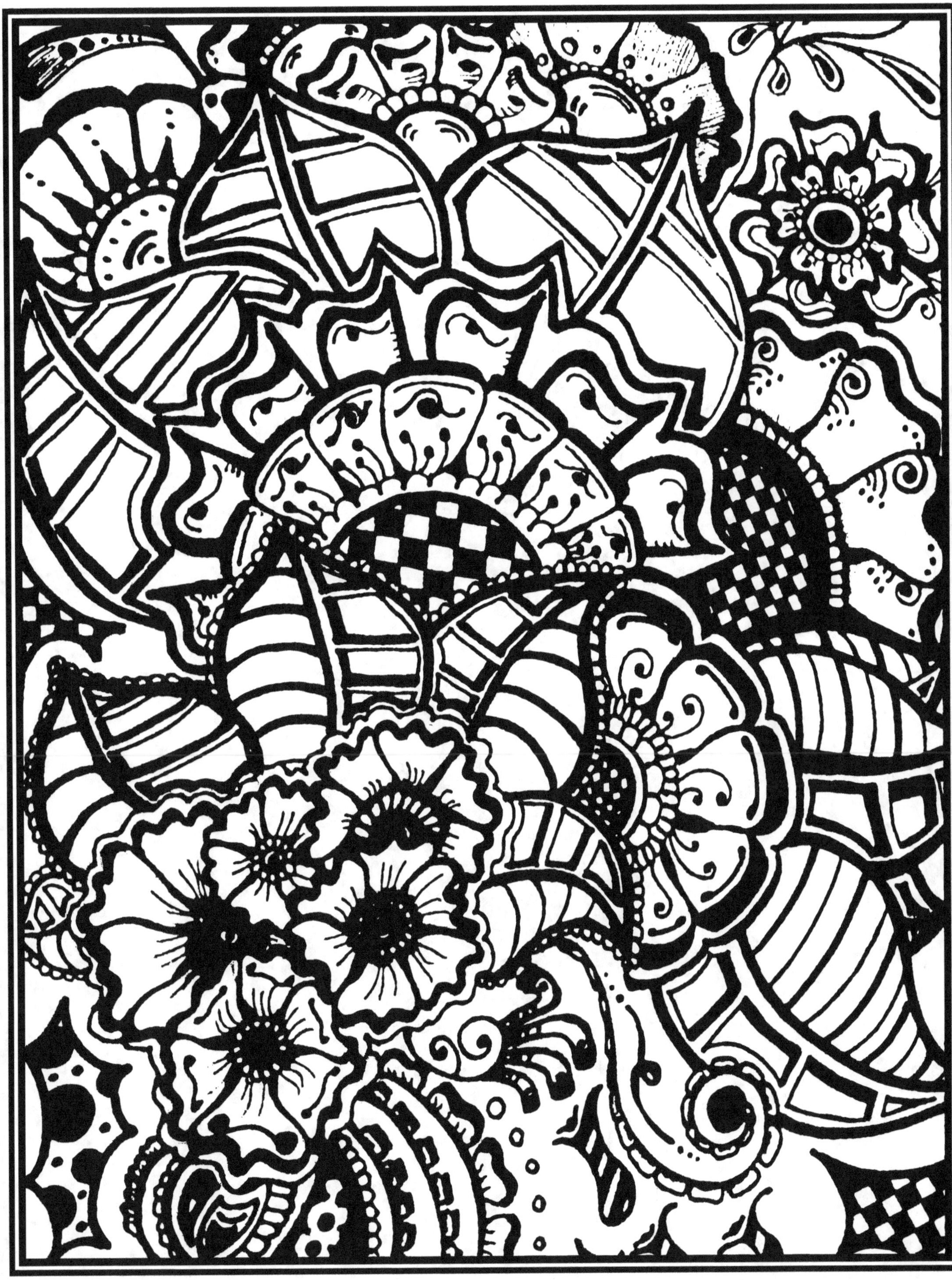

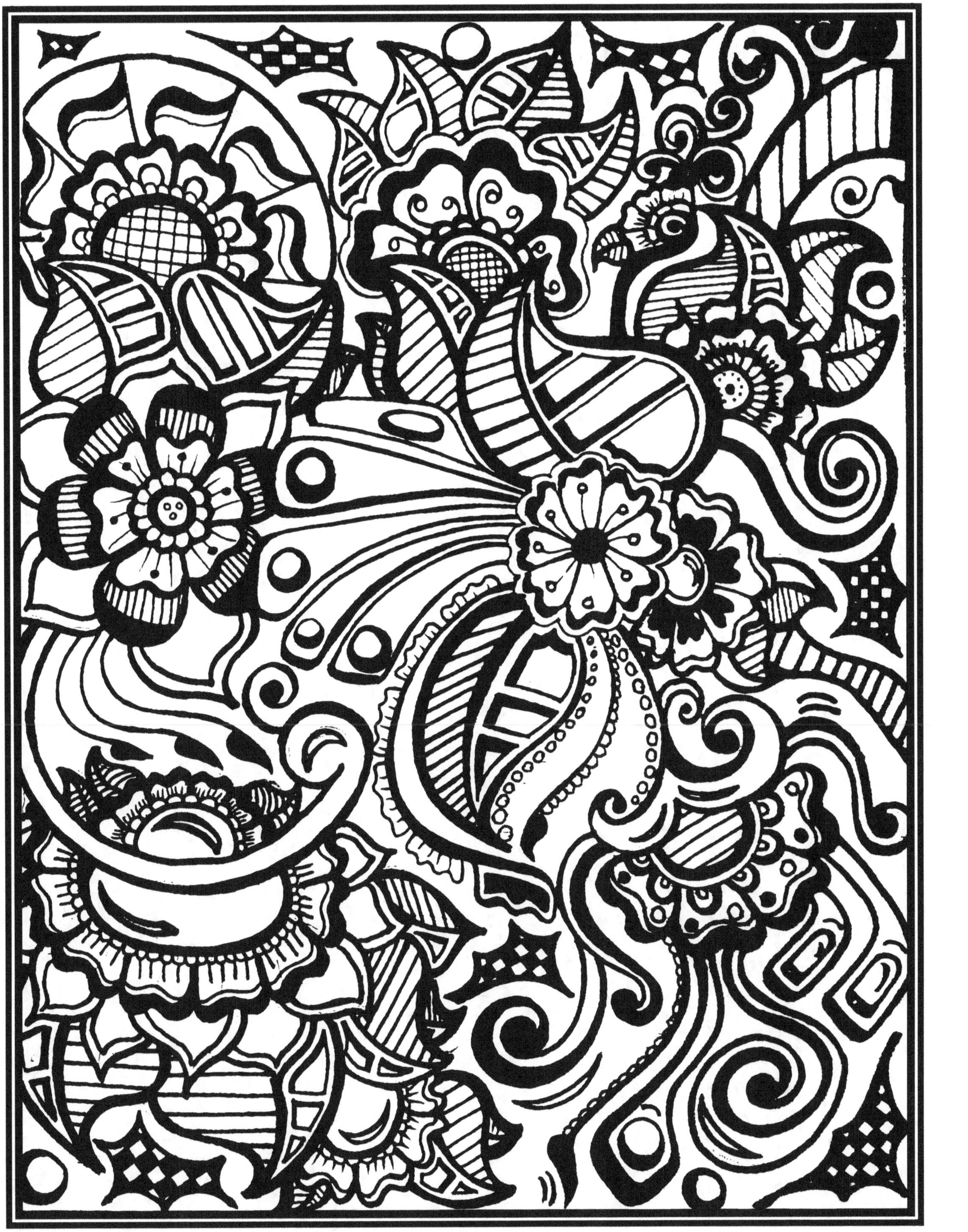

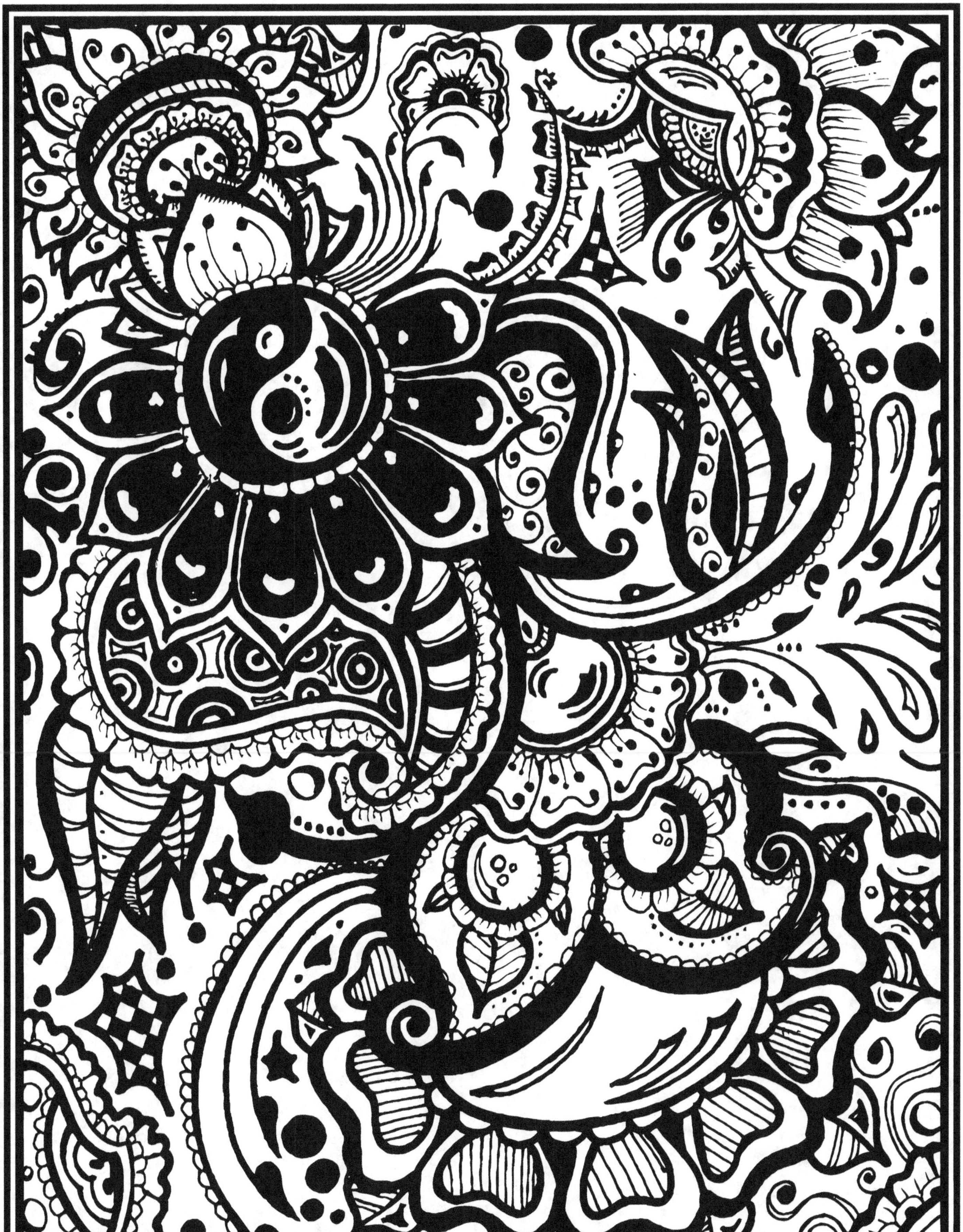

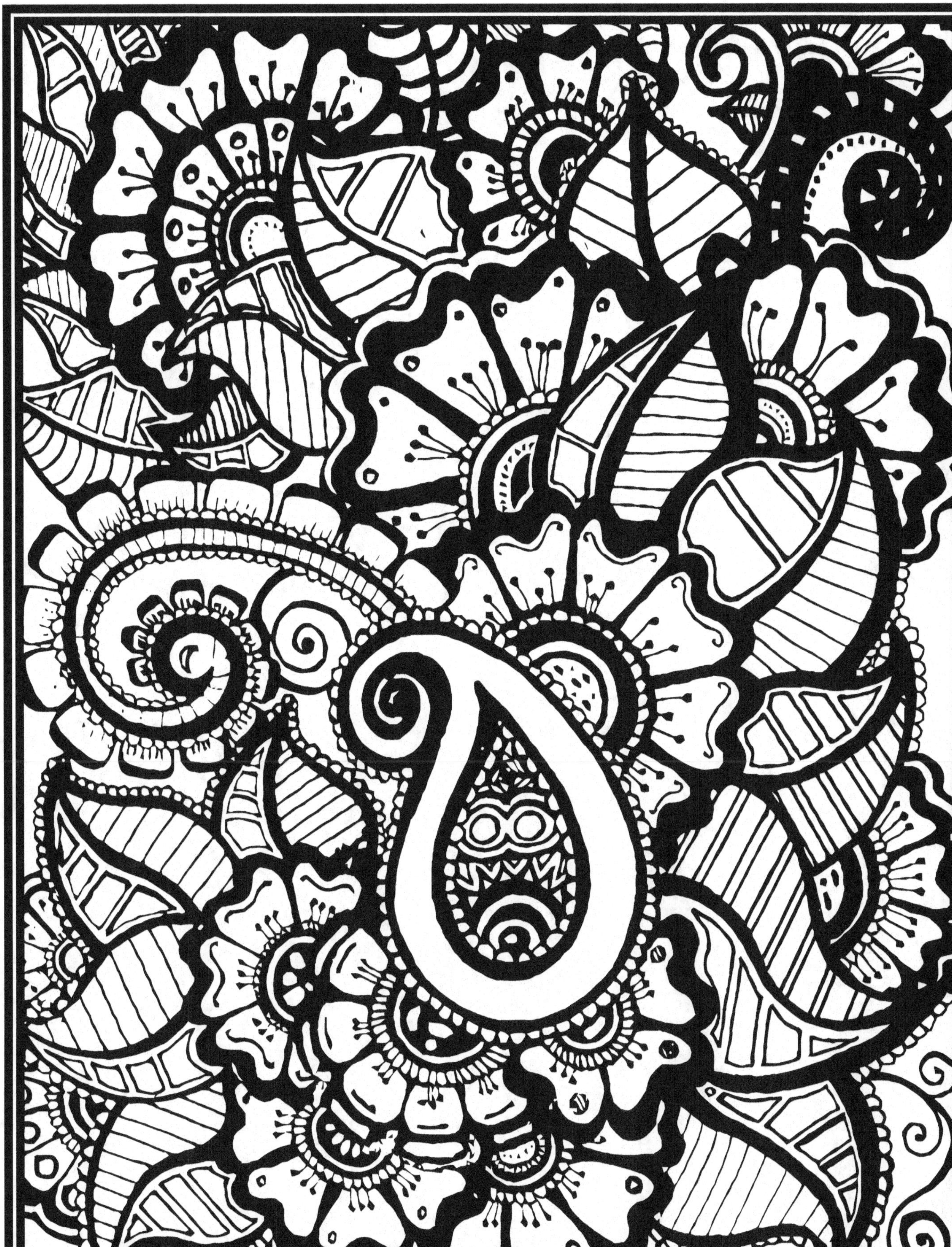

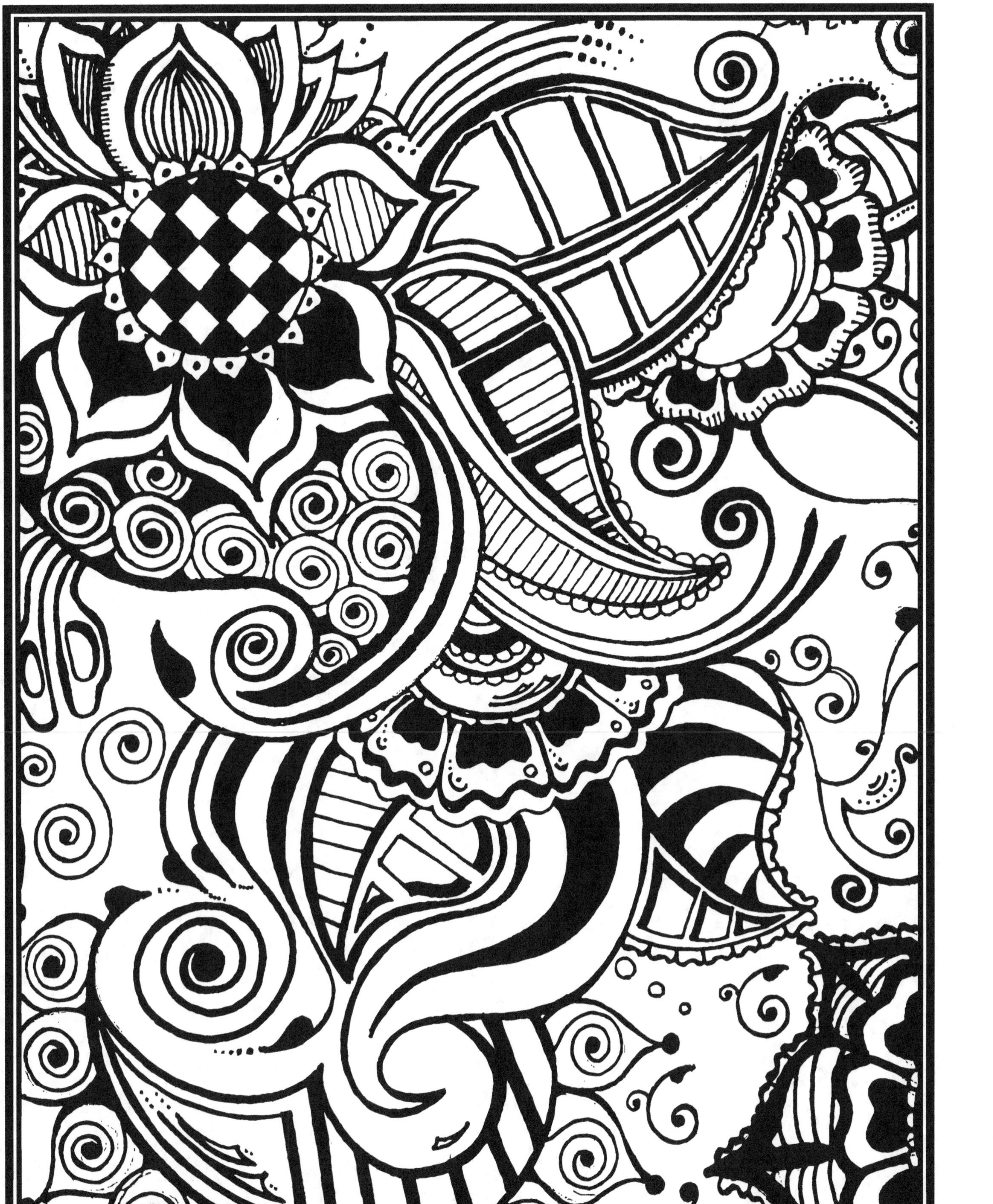

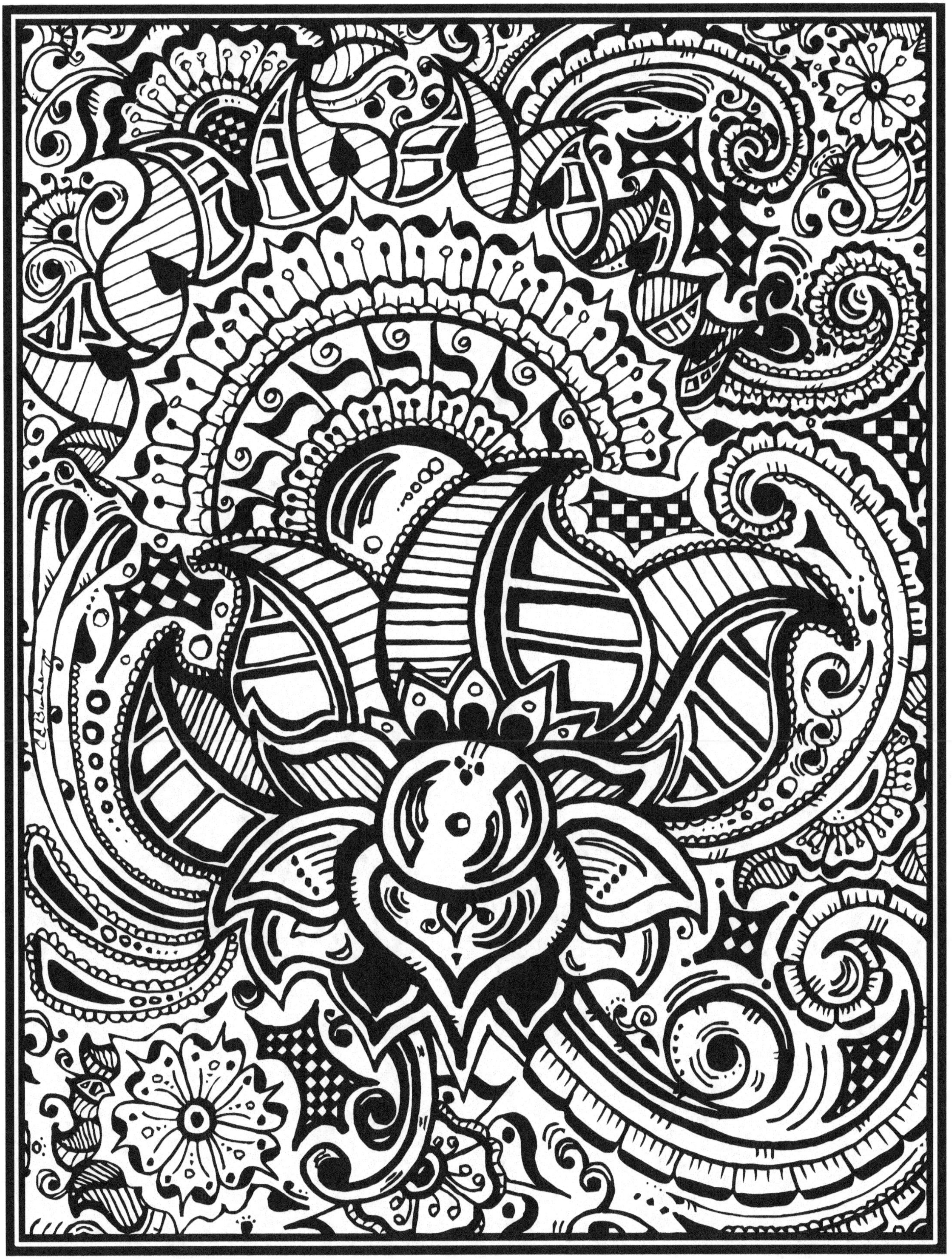

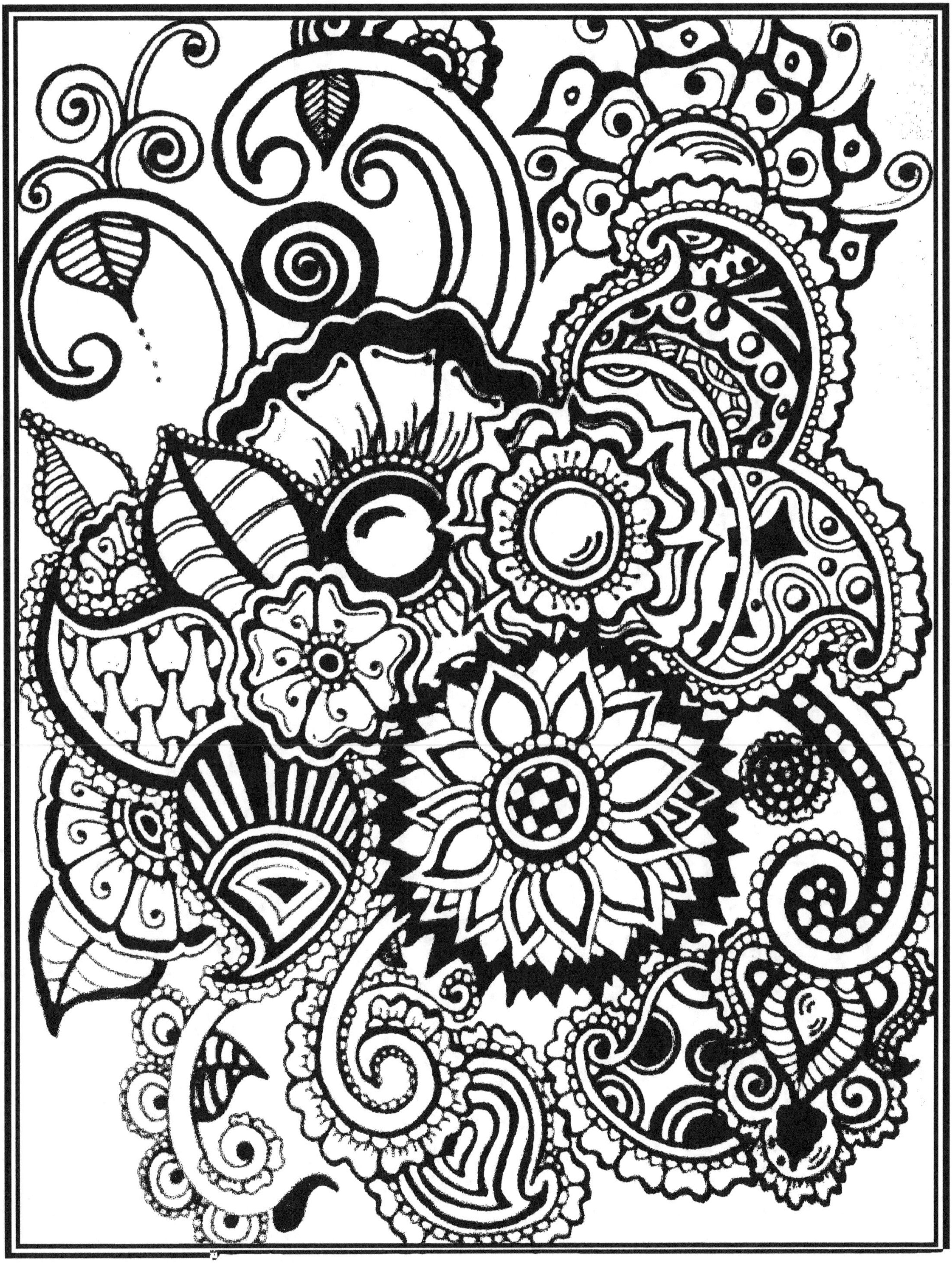

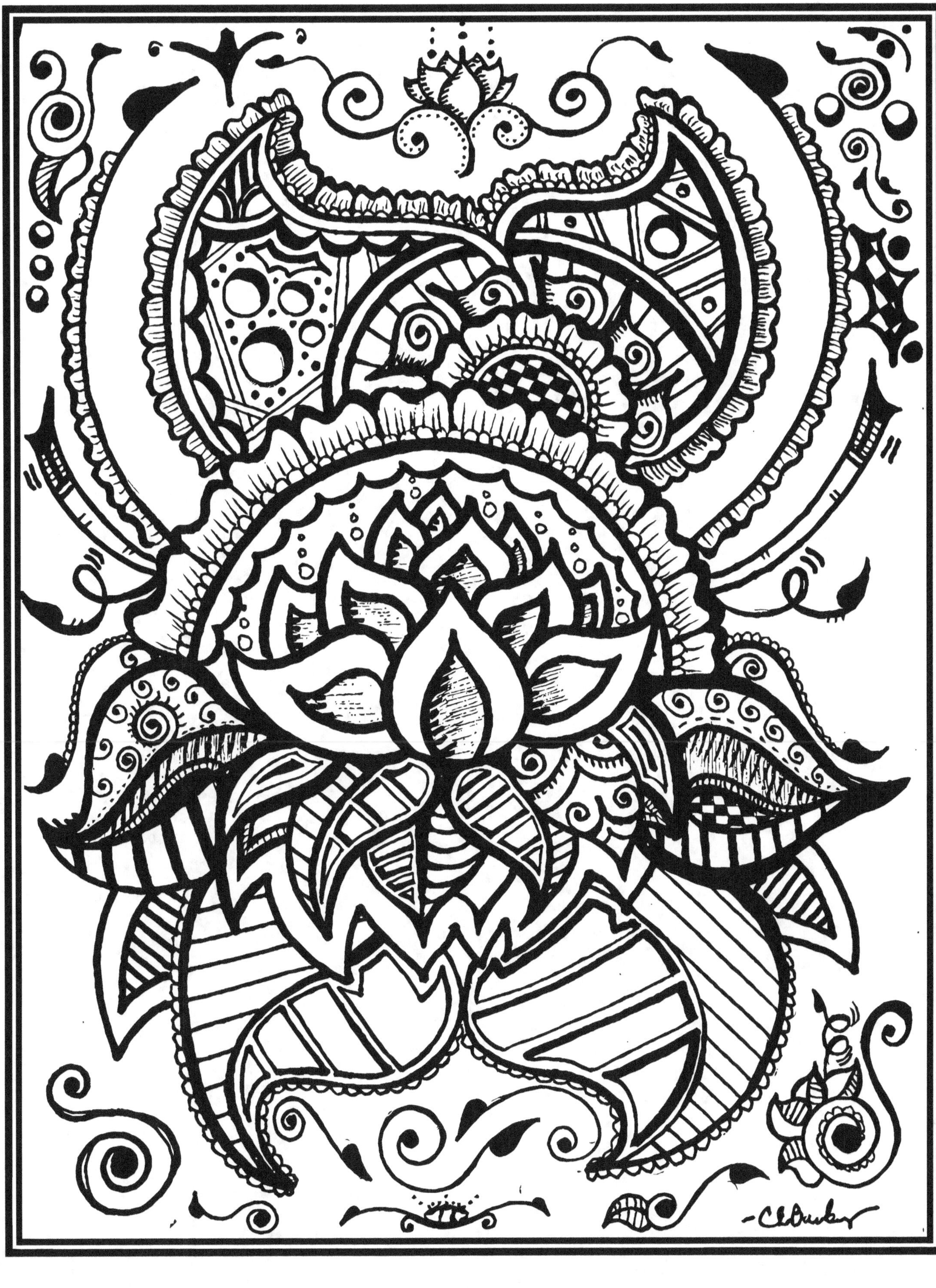

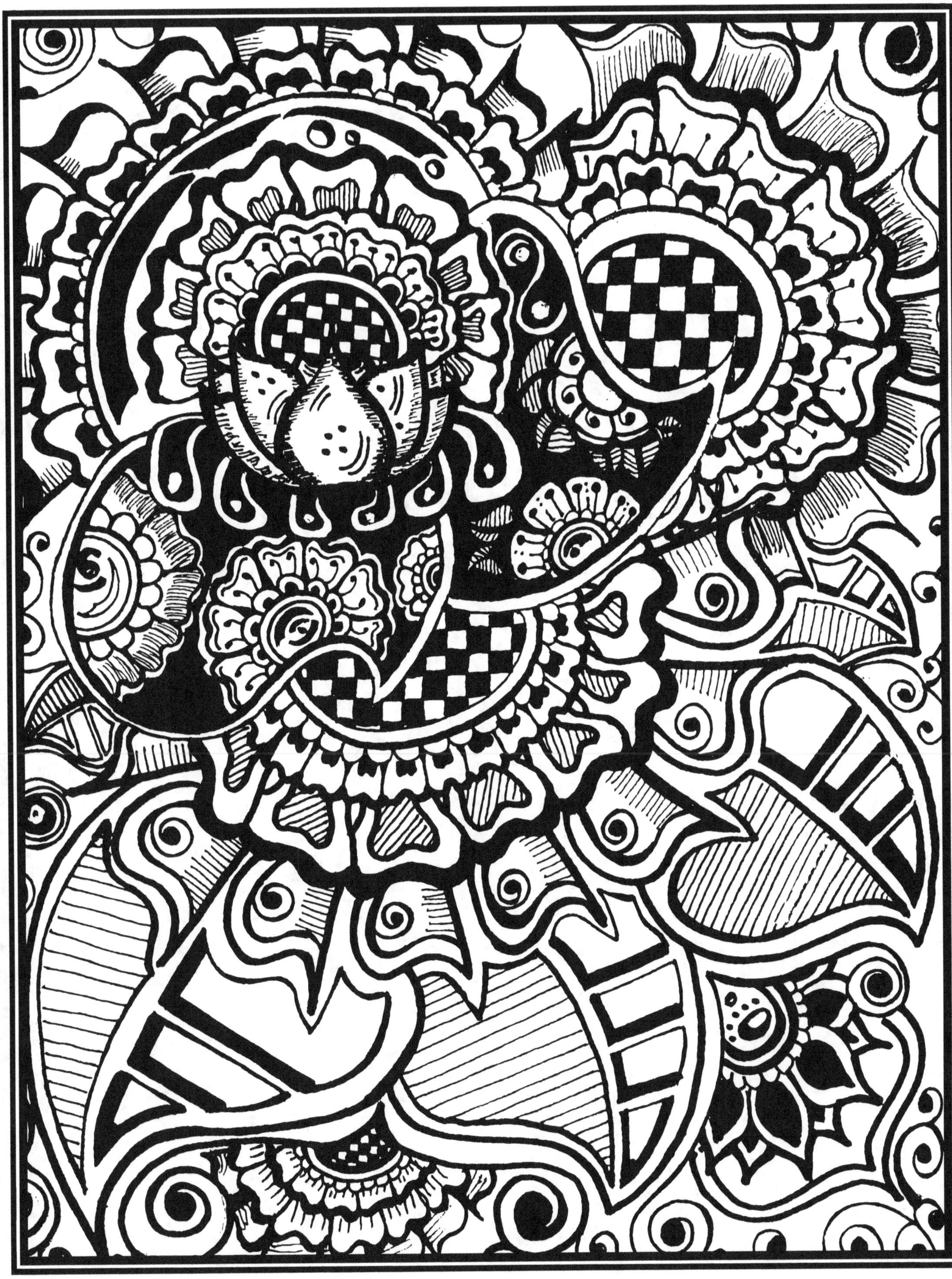

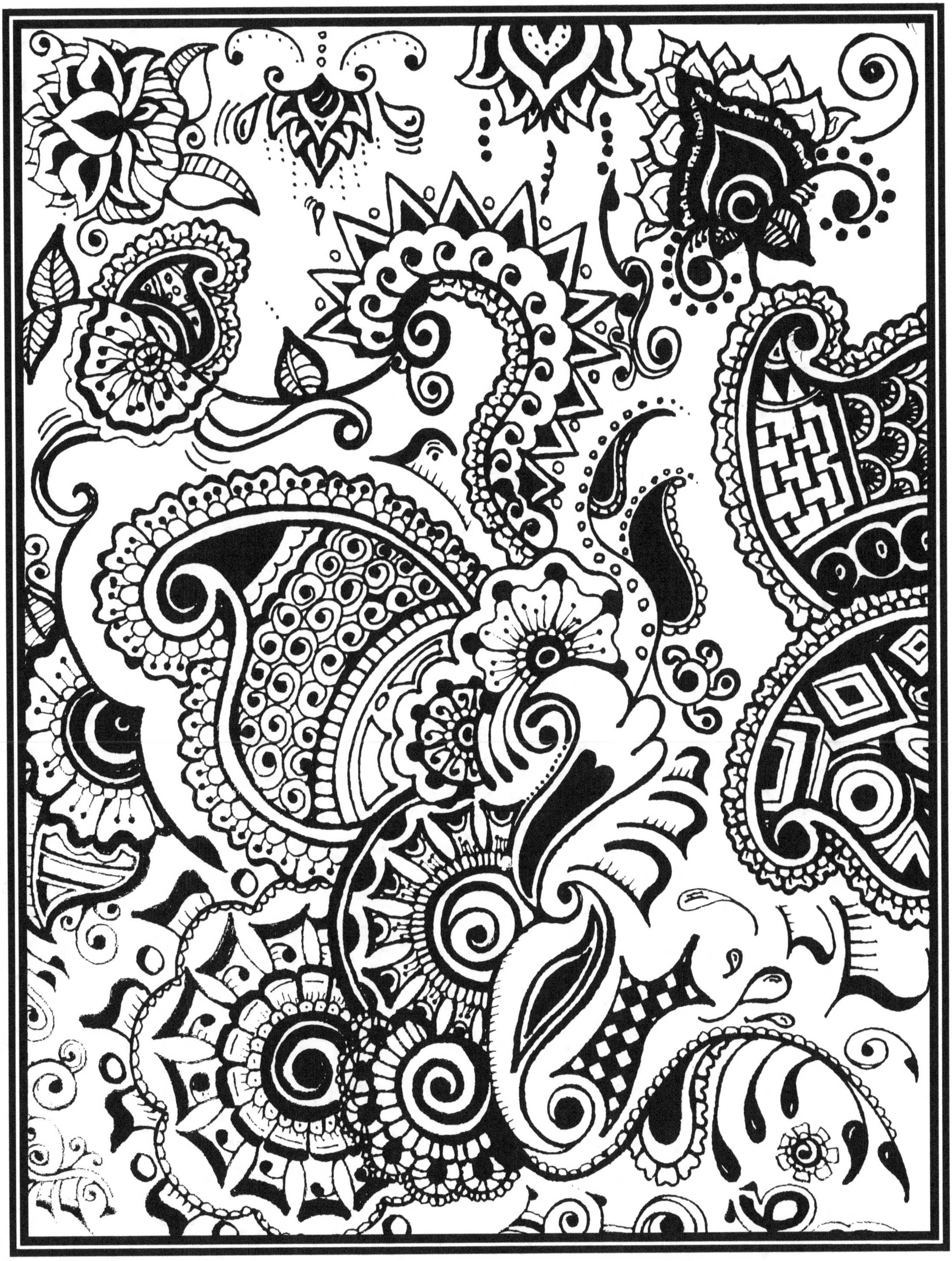

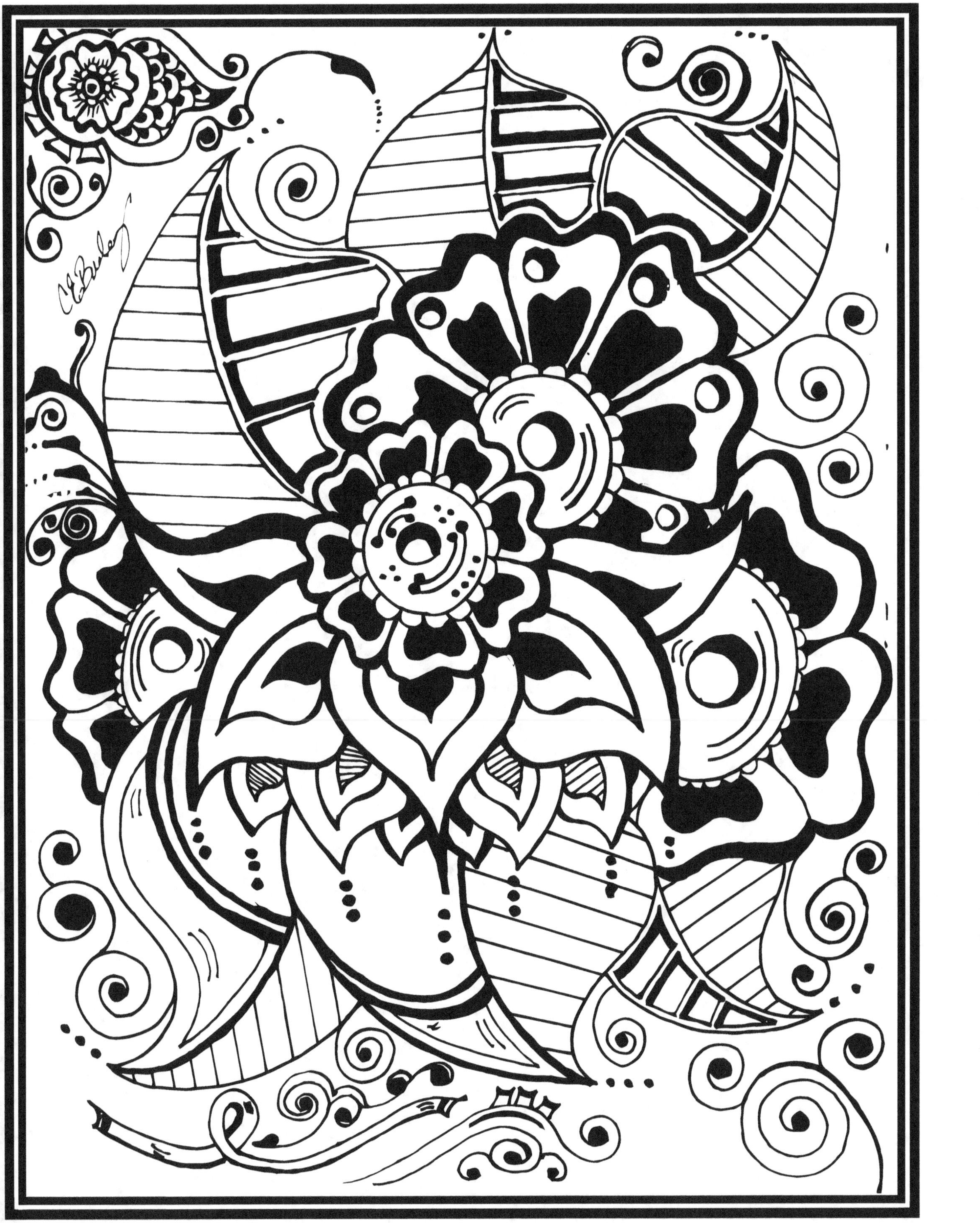

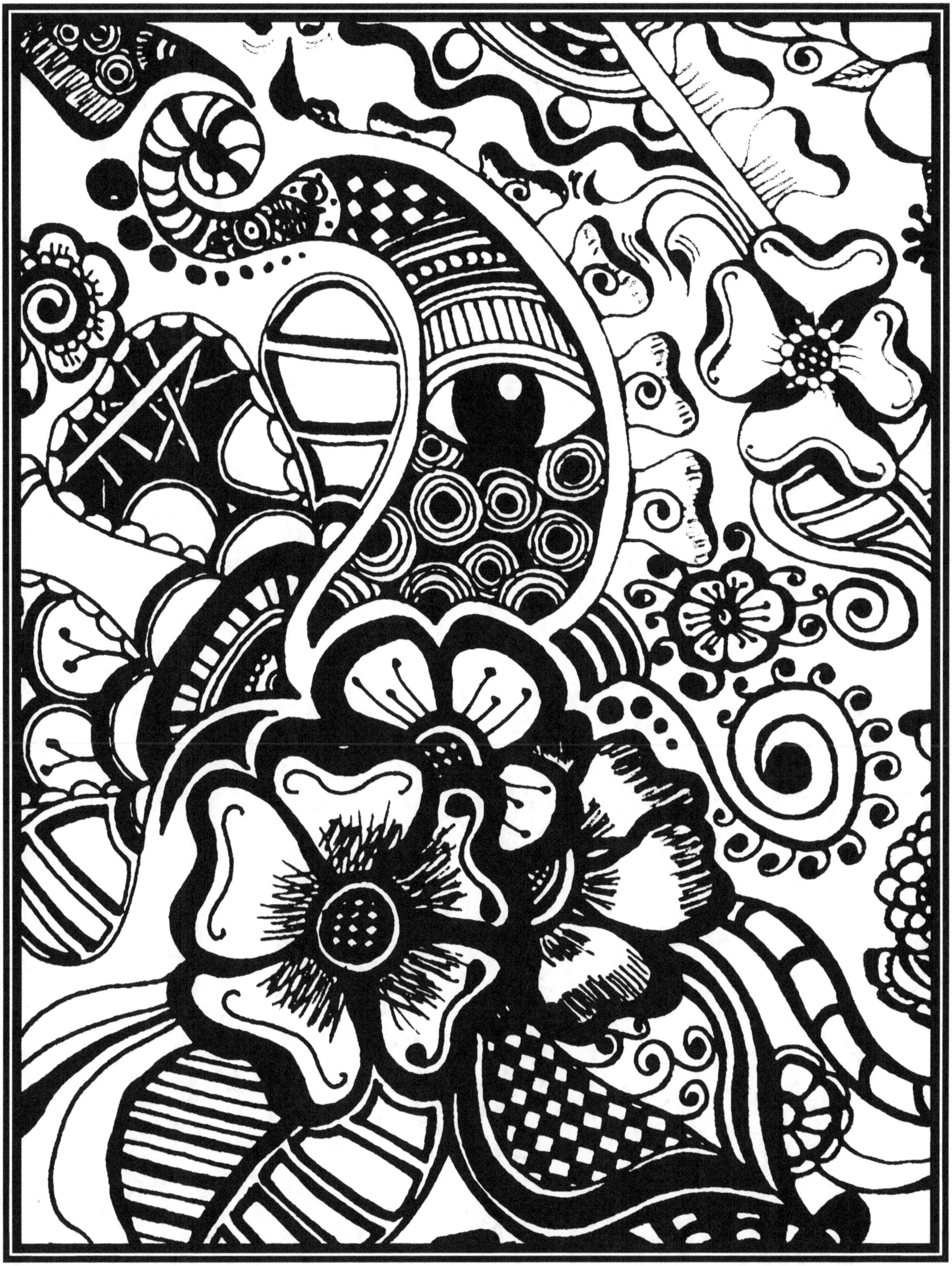

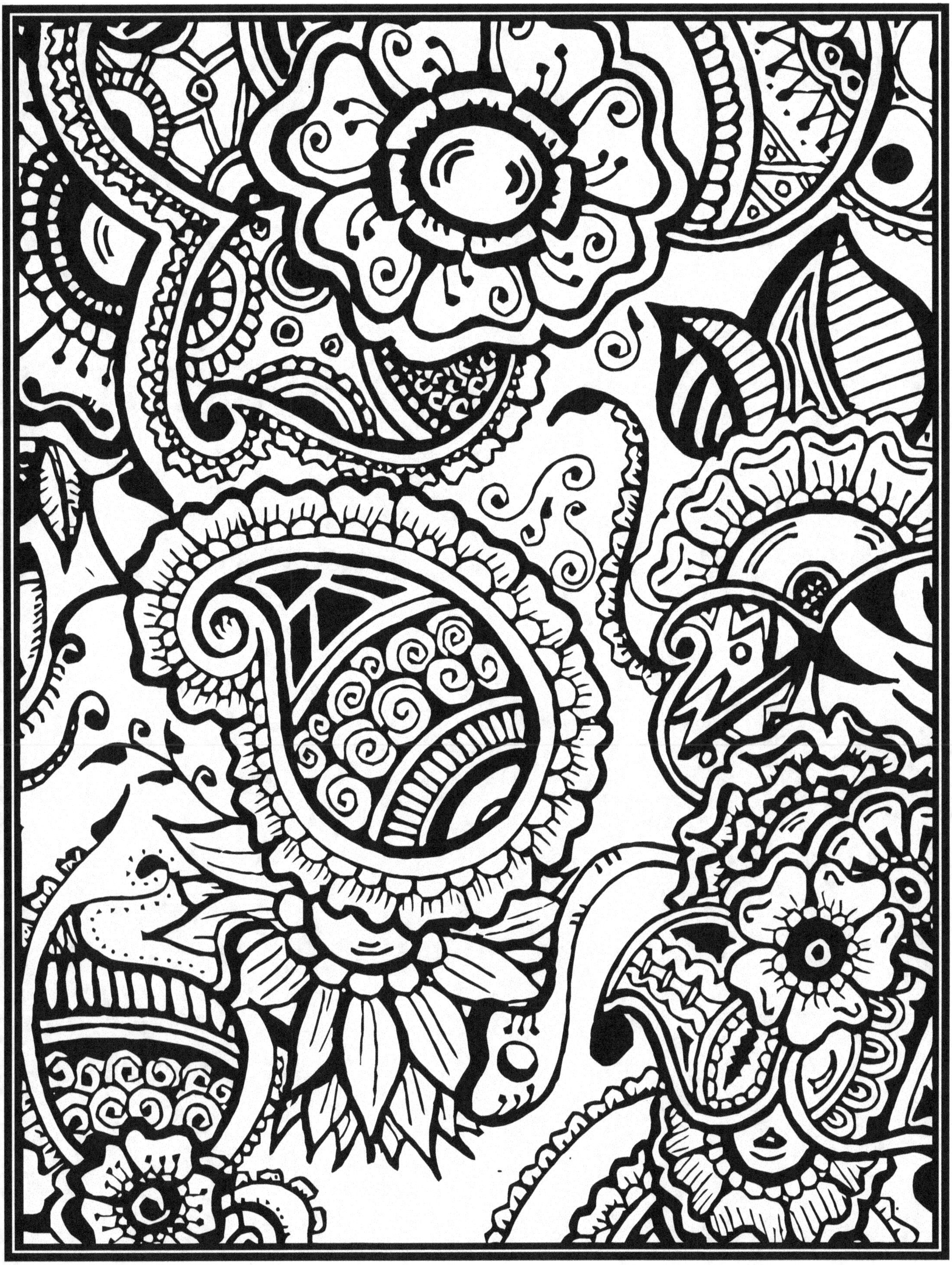

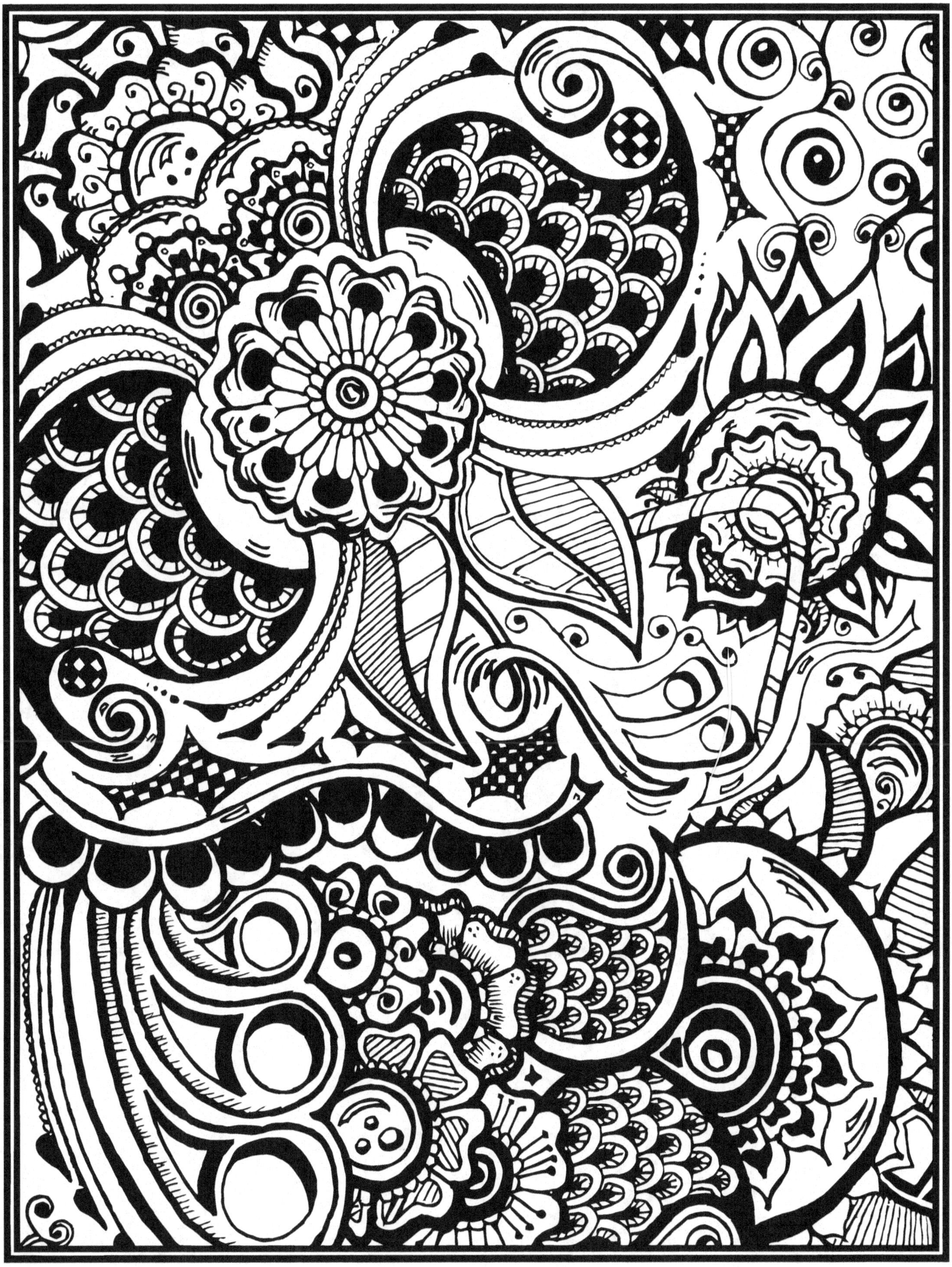

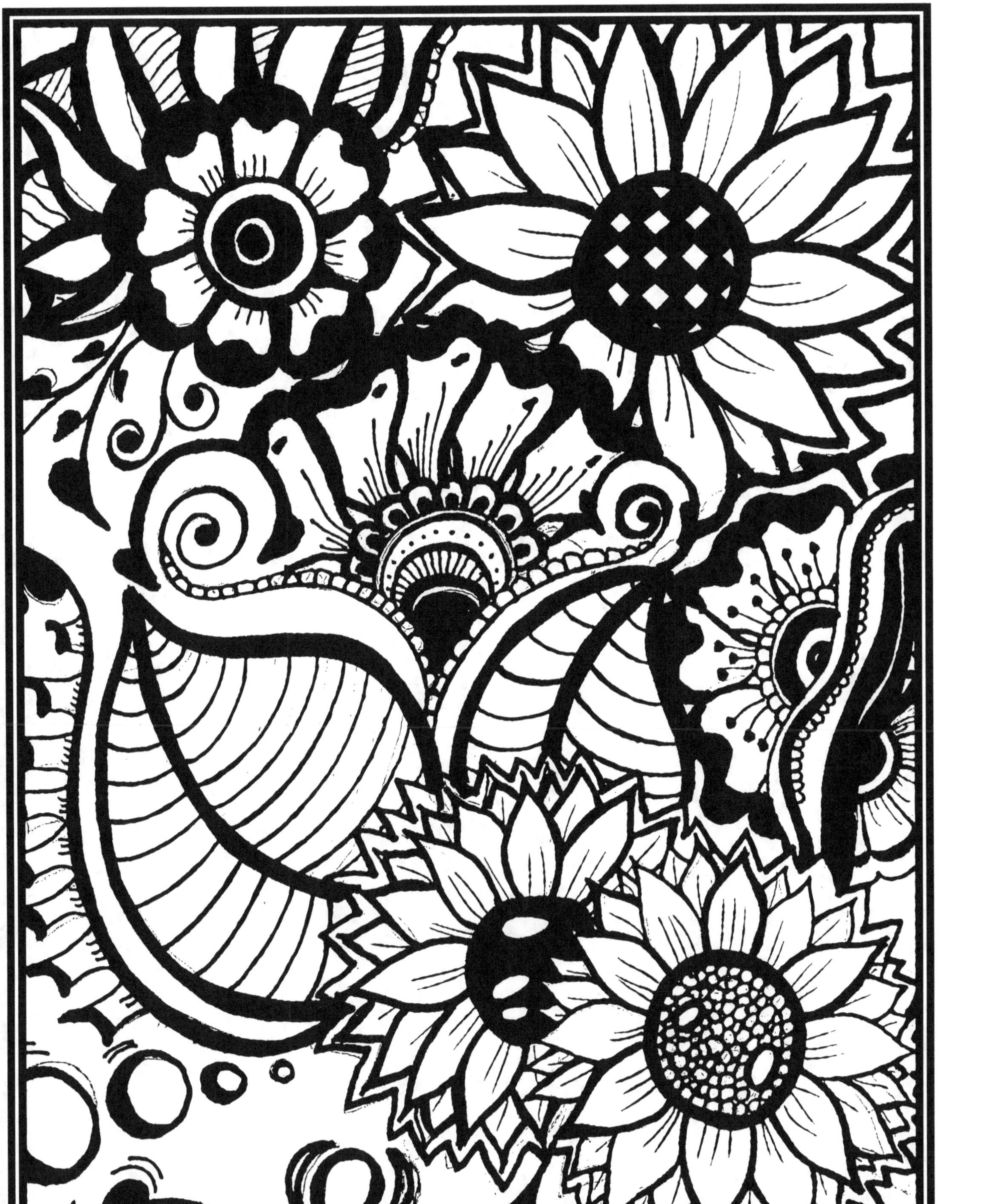

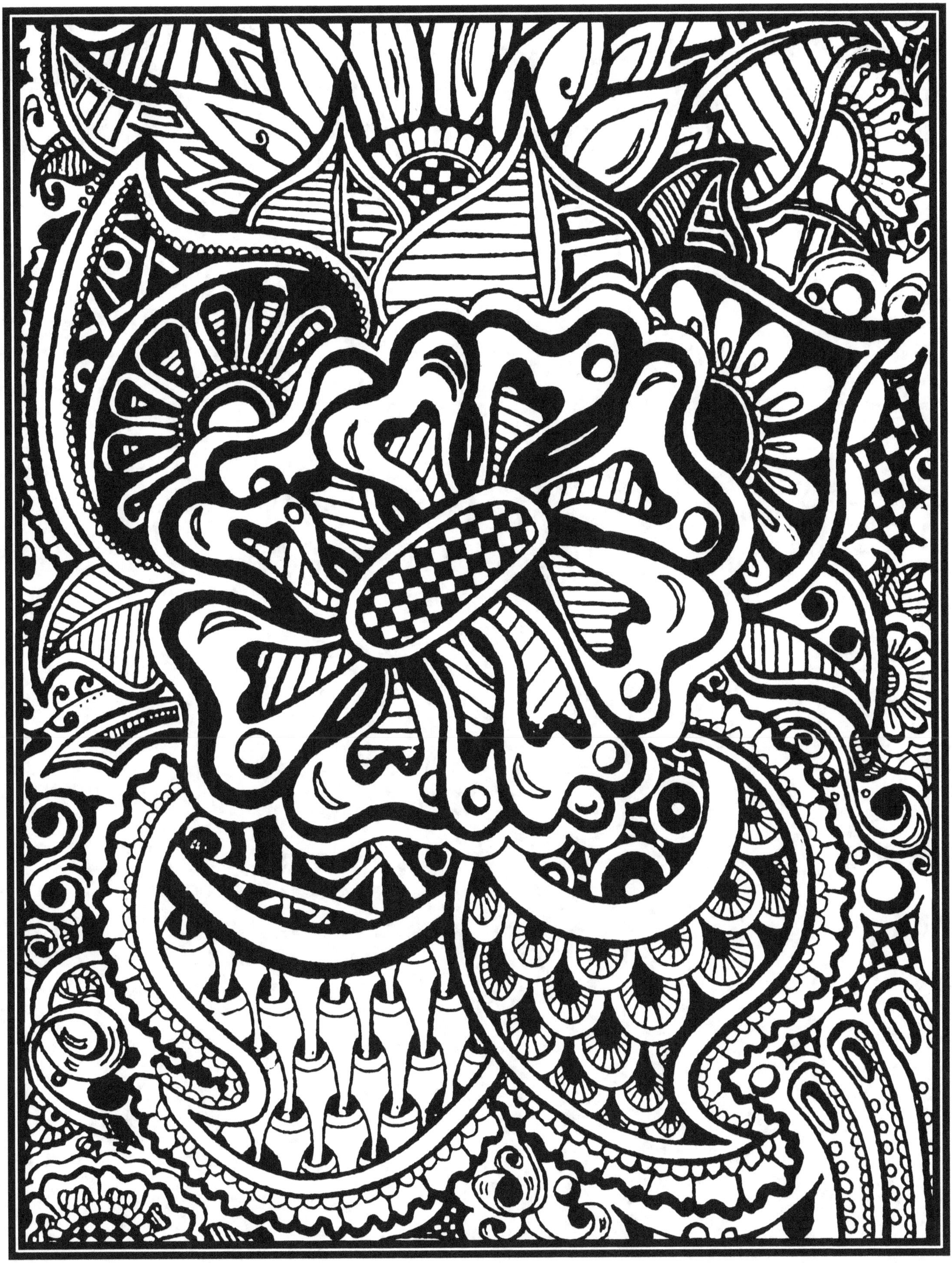

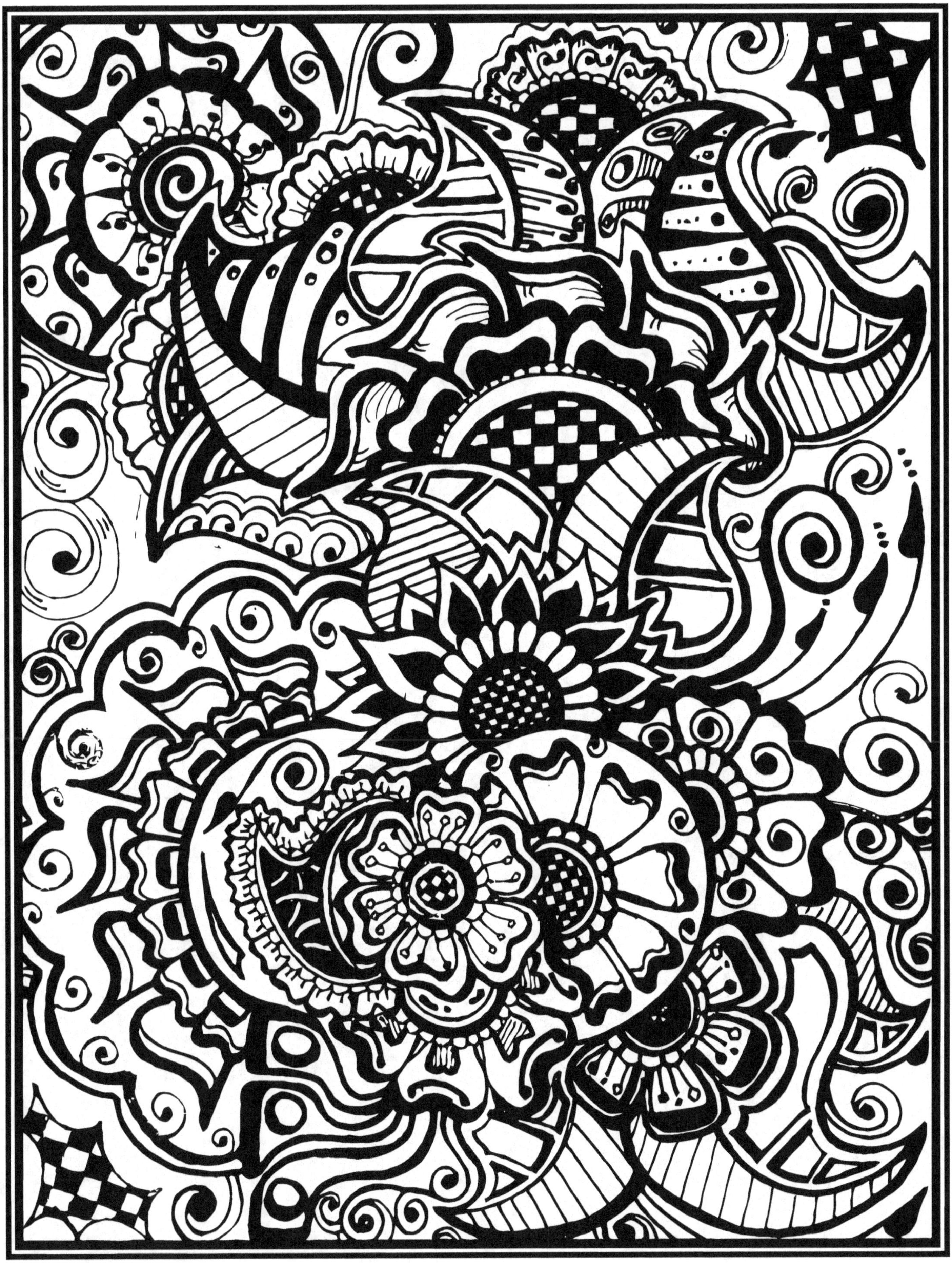

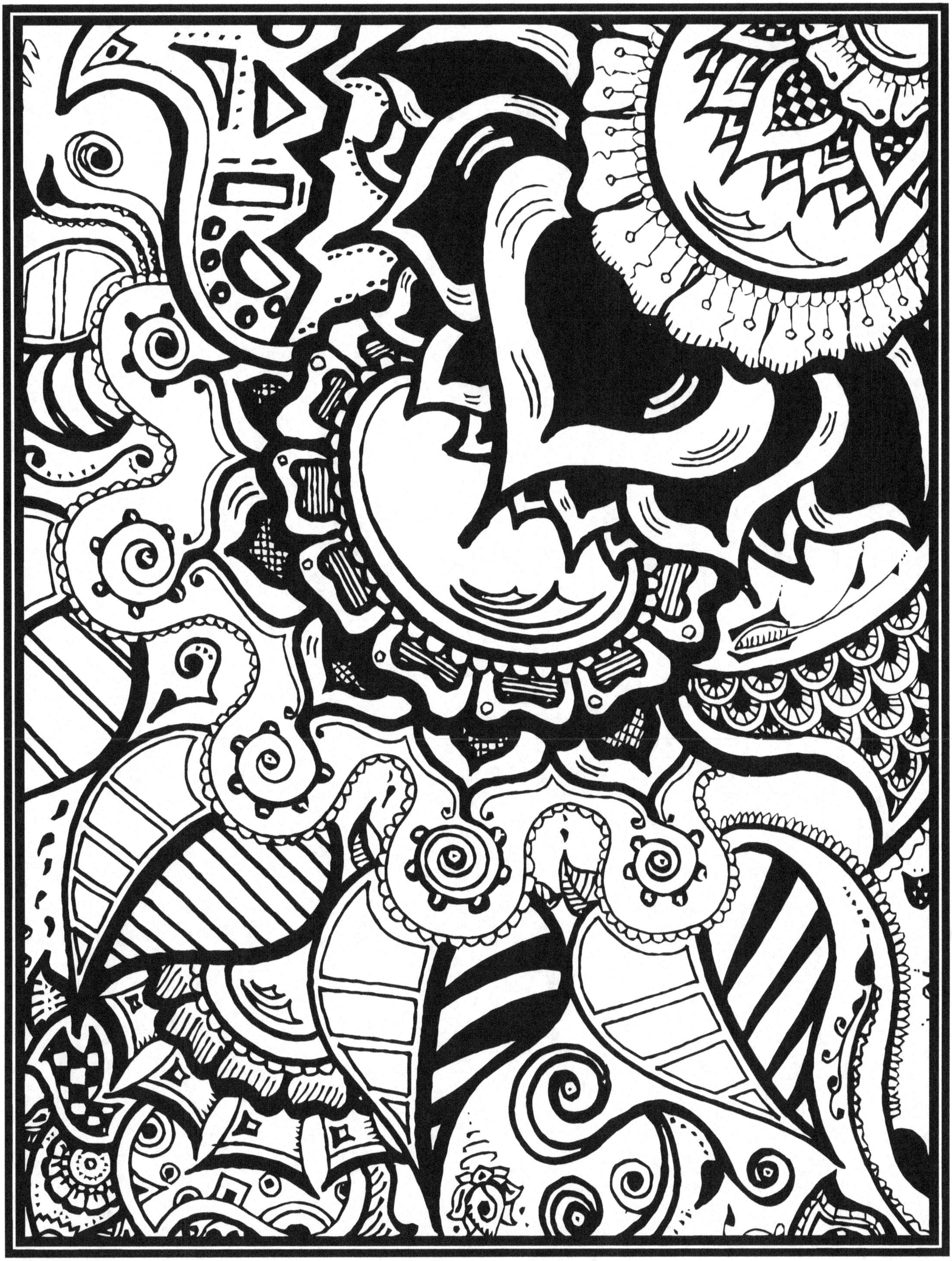

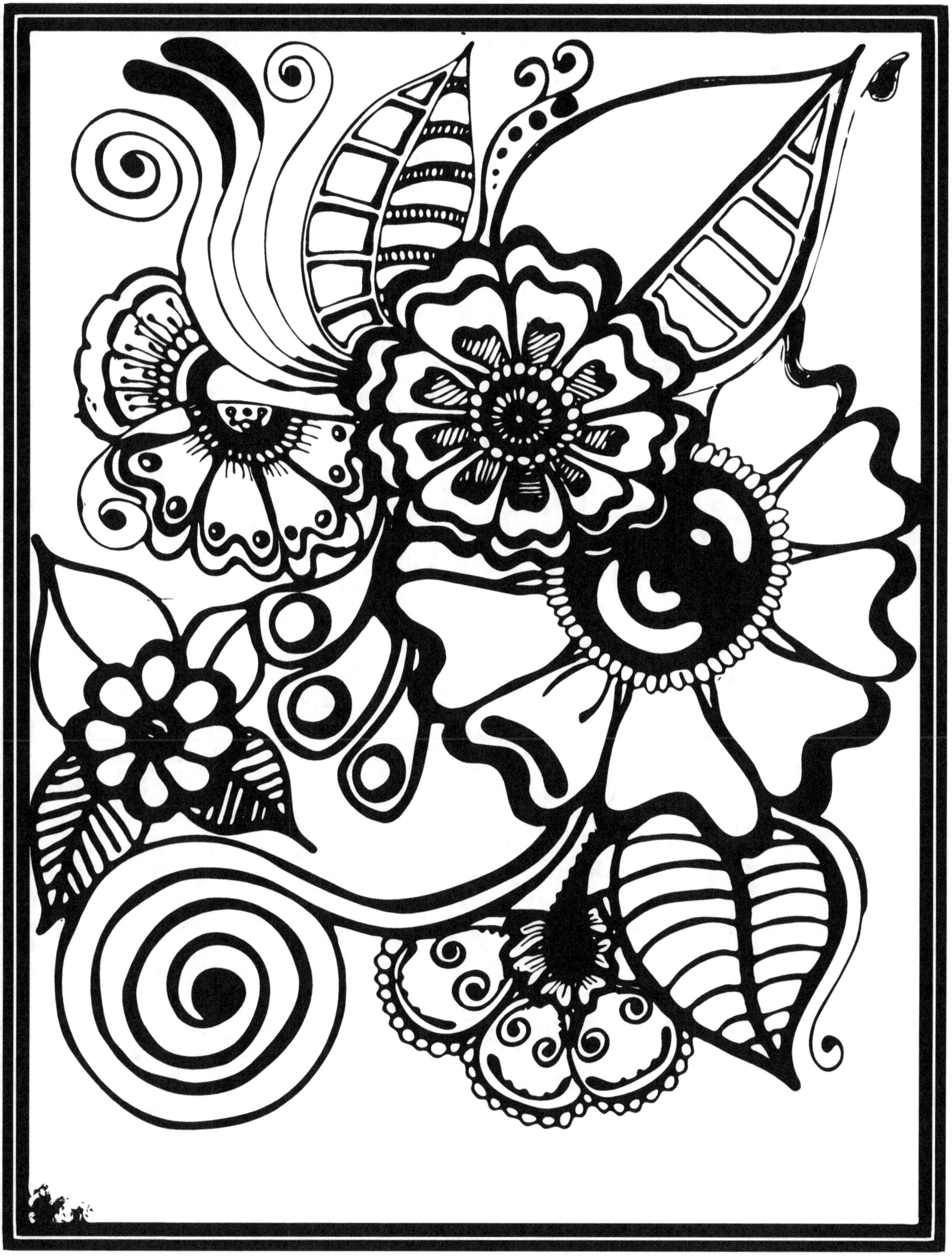

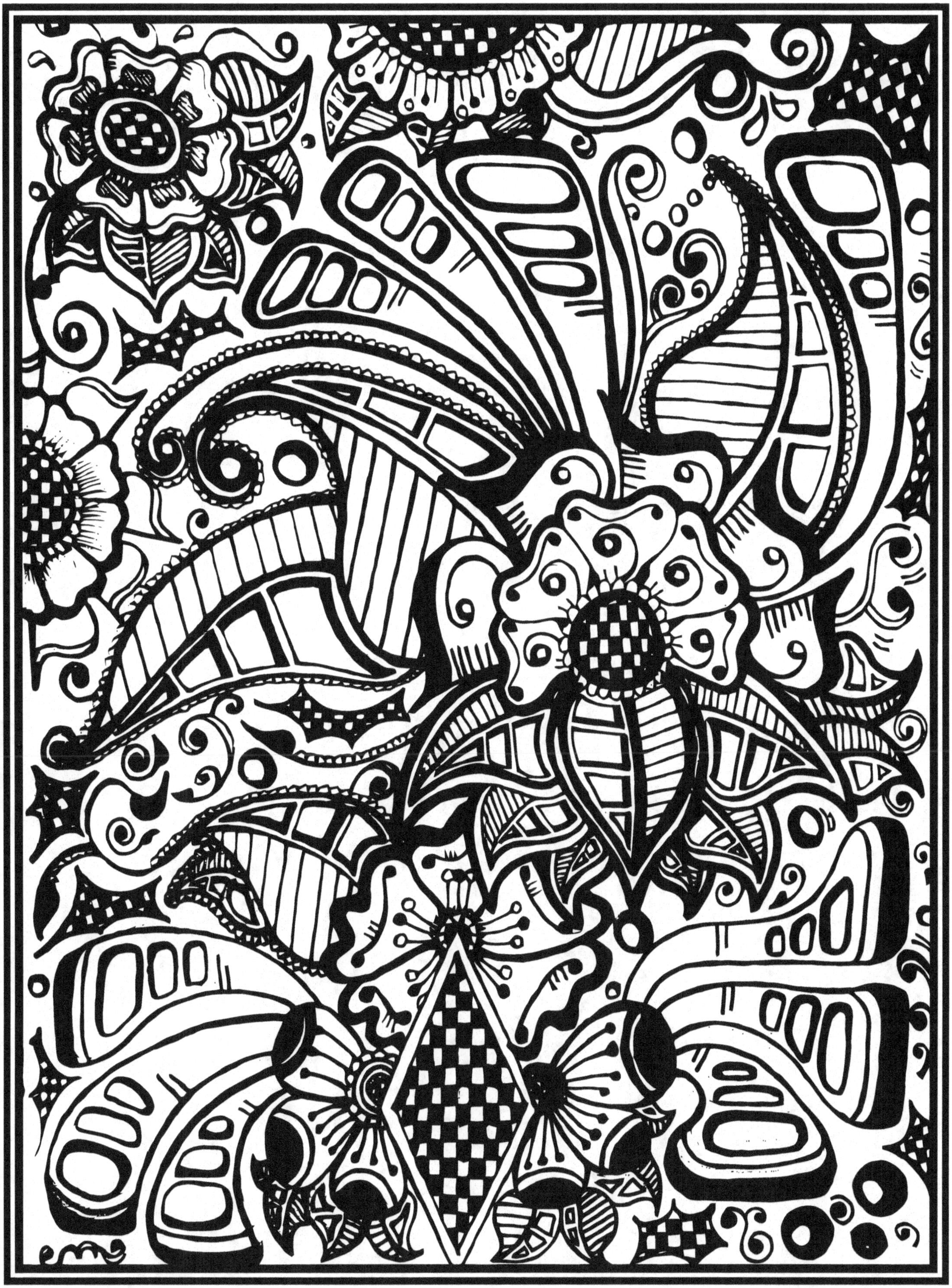

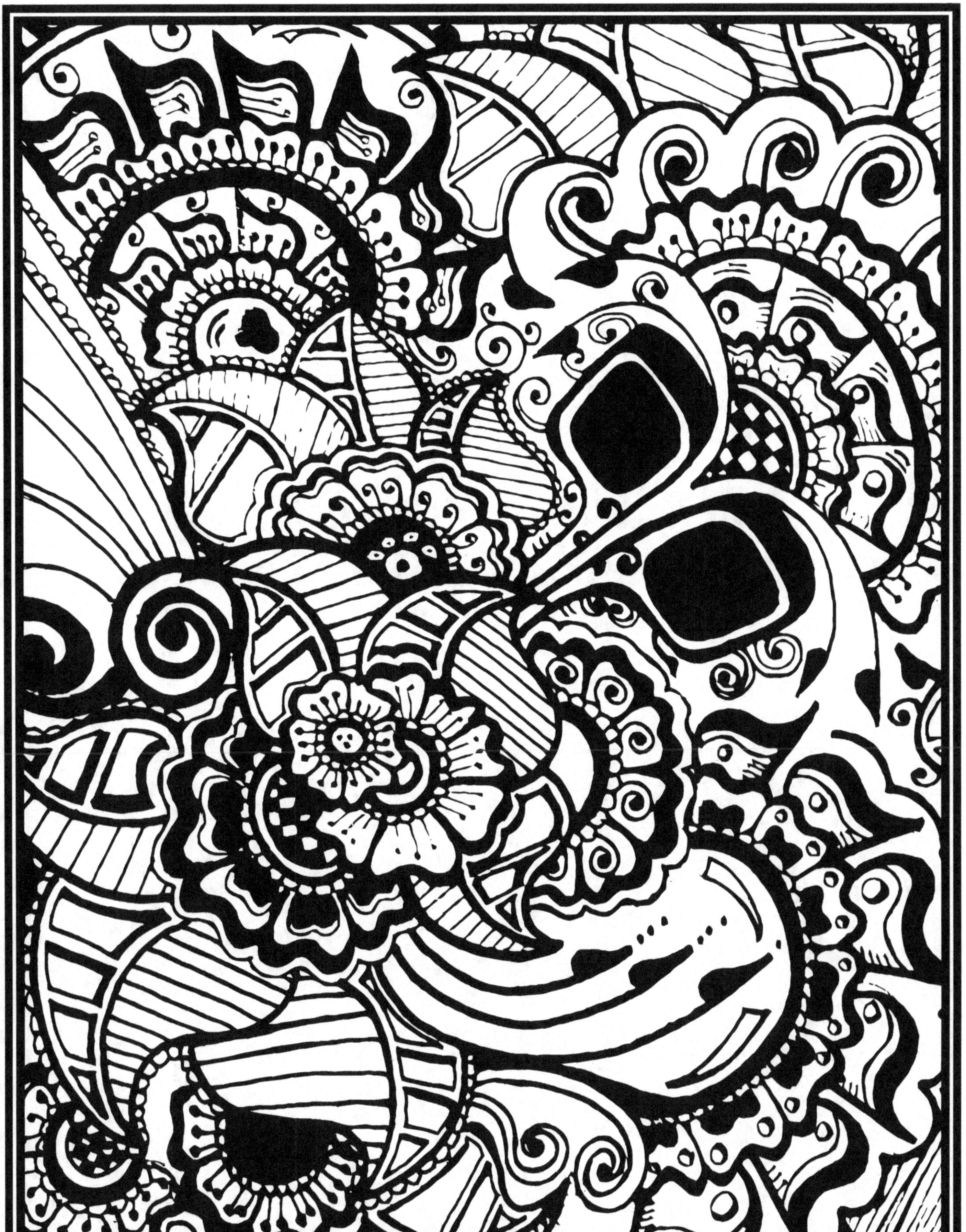

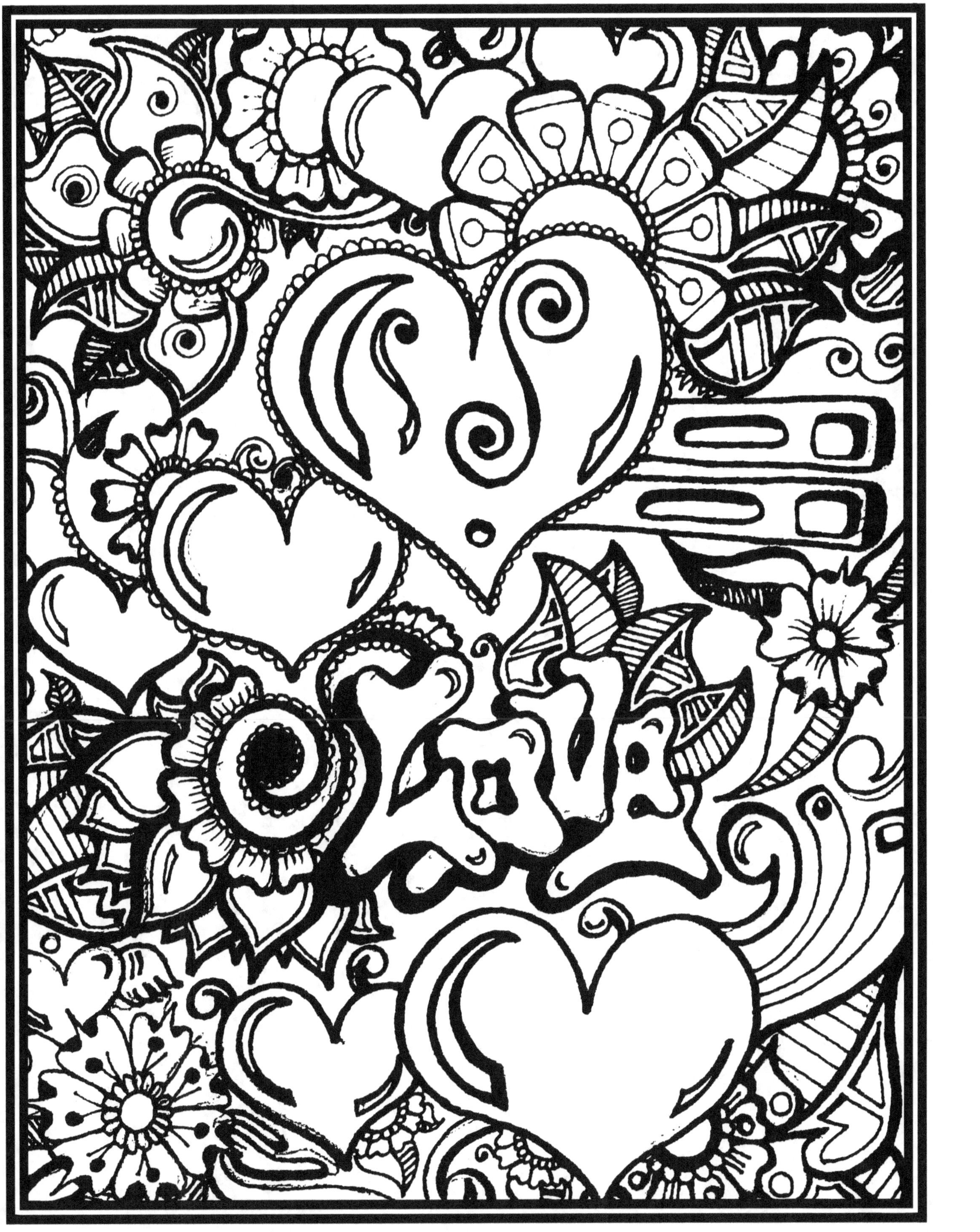
Love

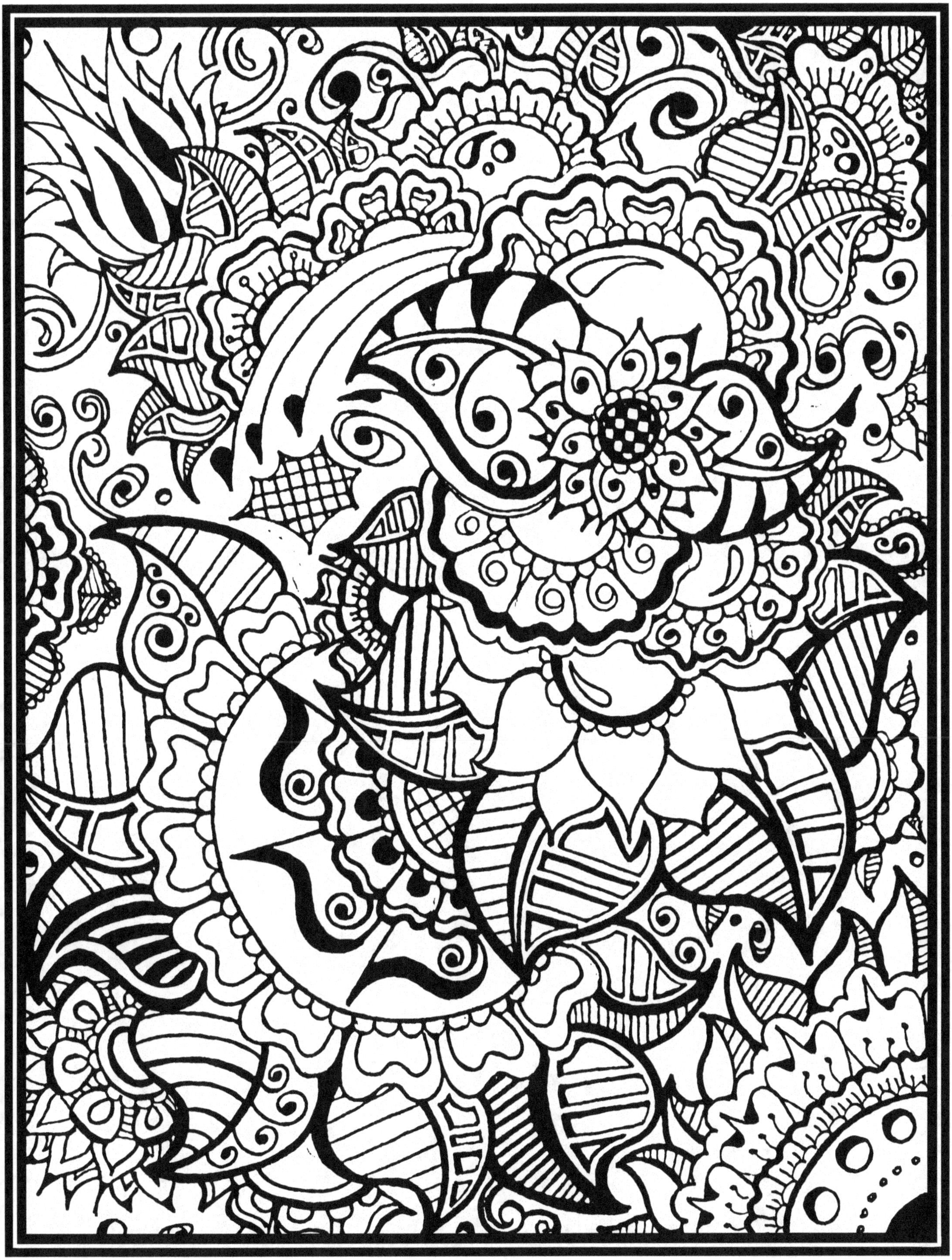

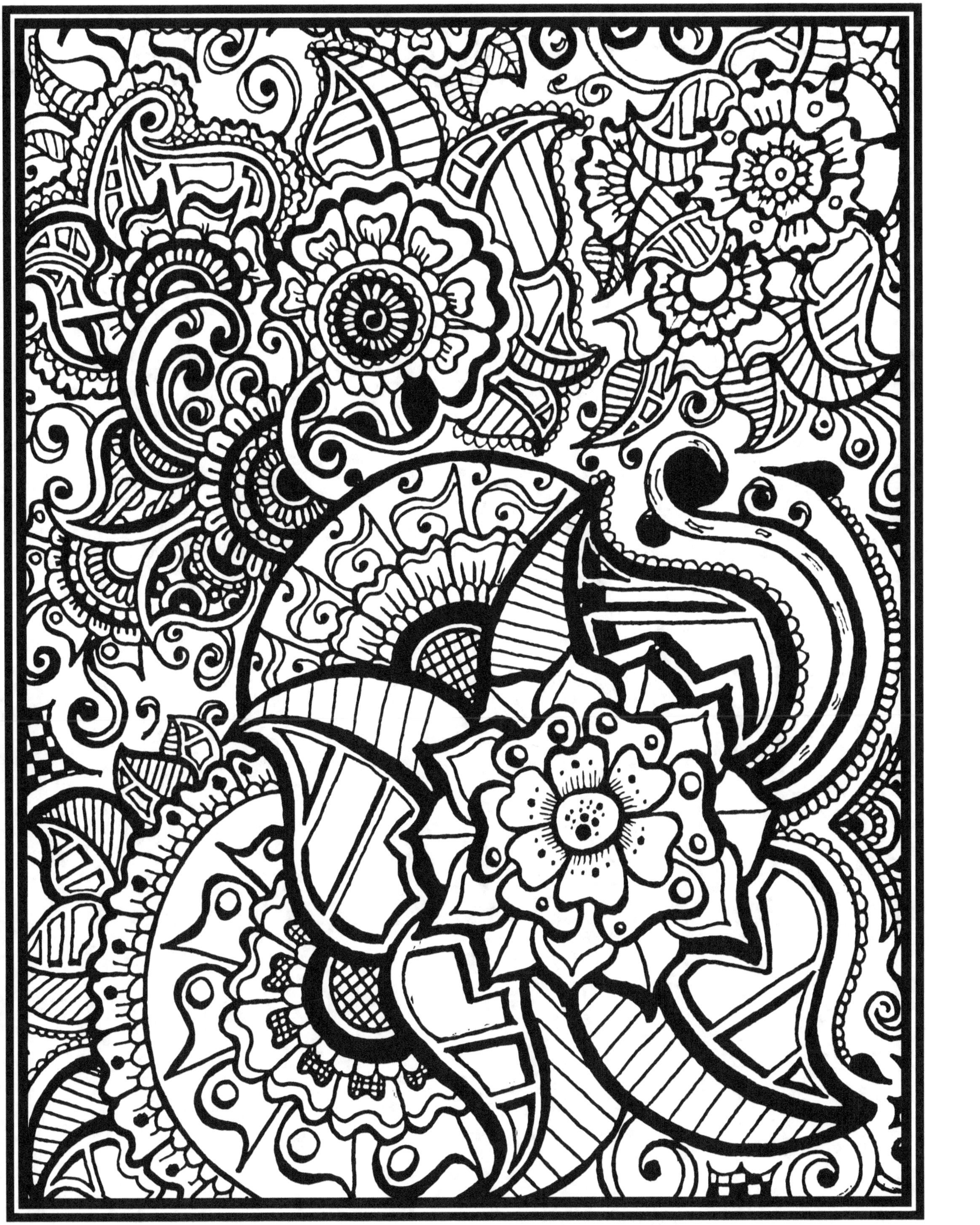

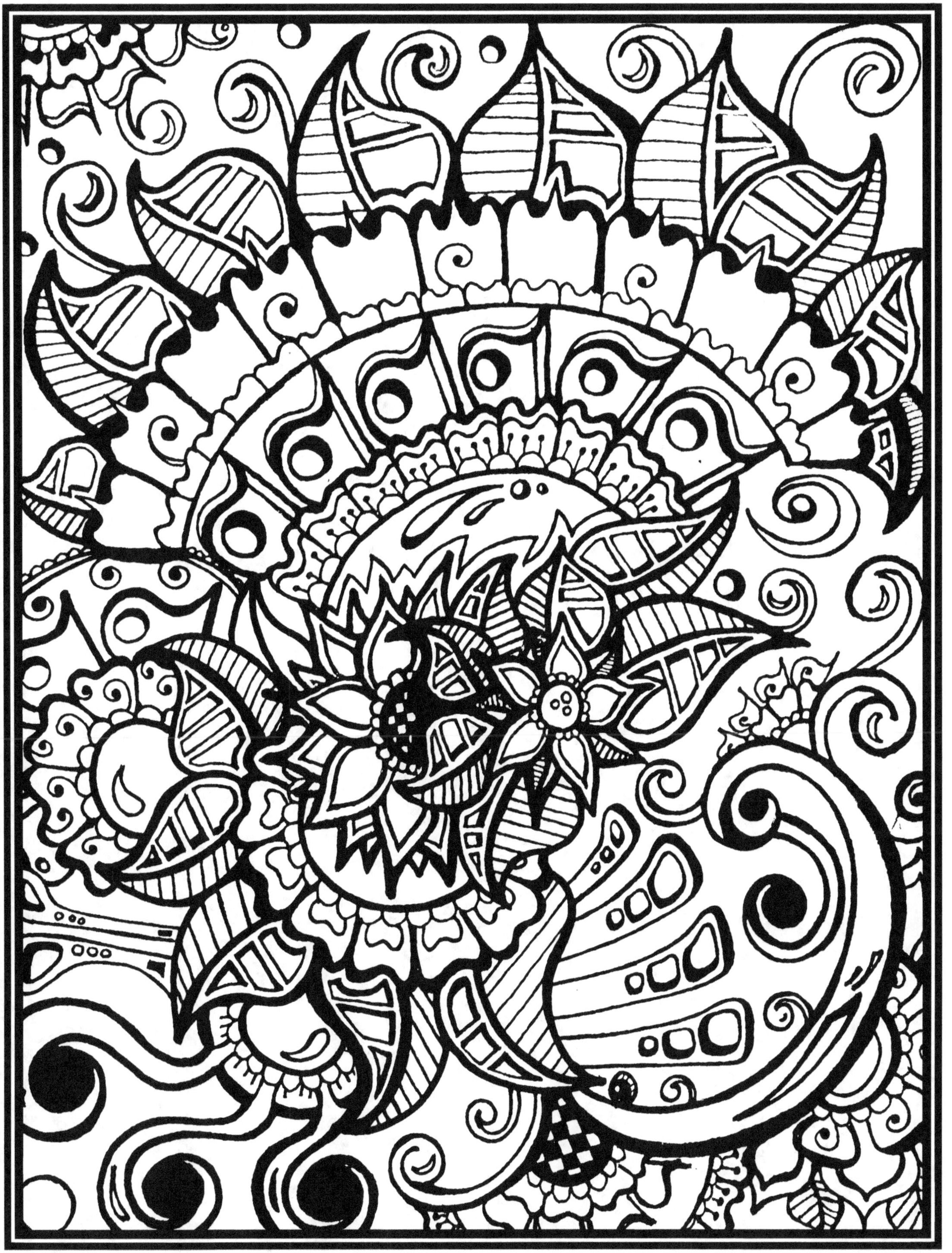

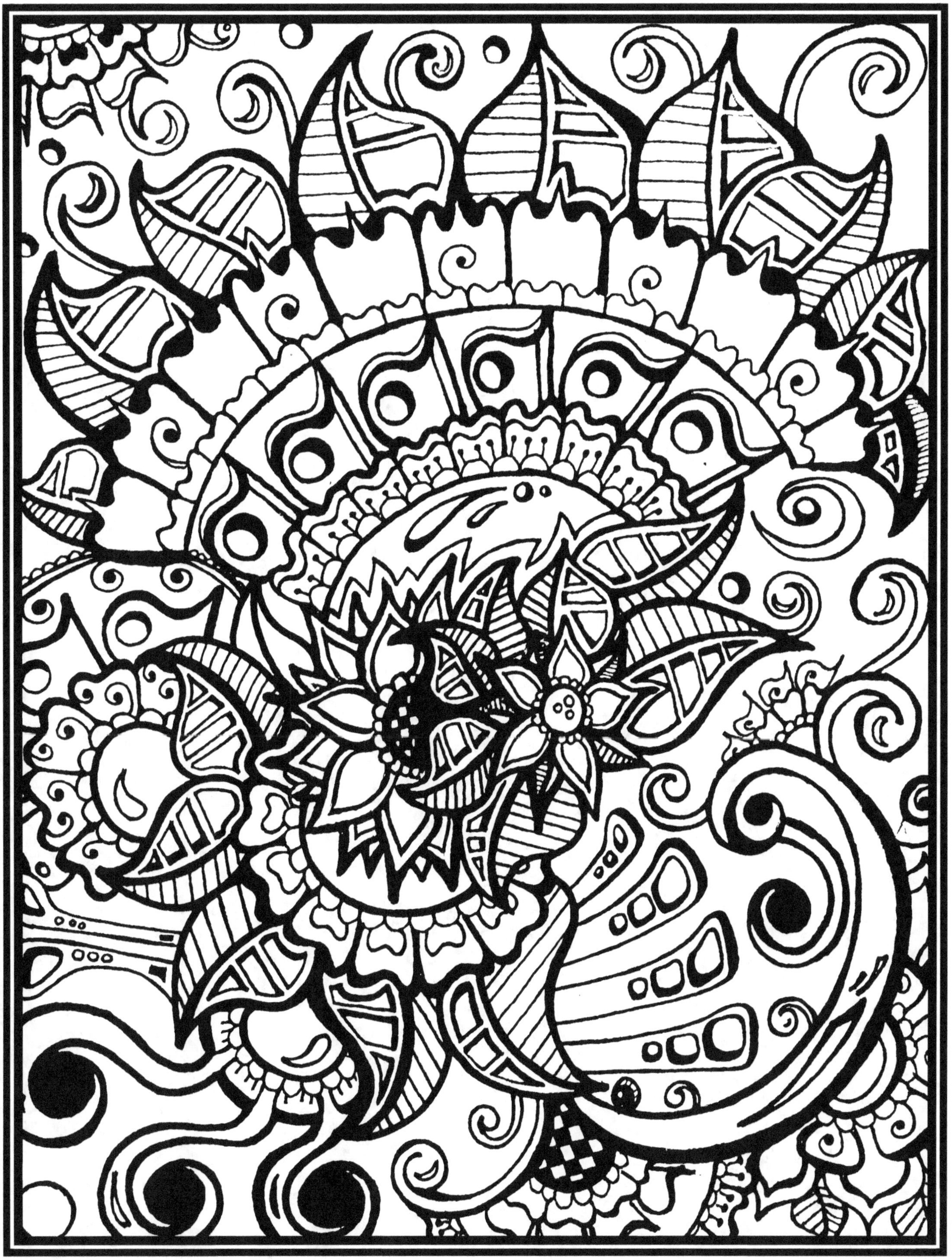

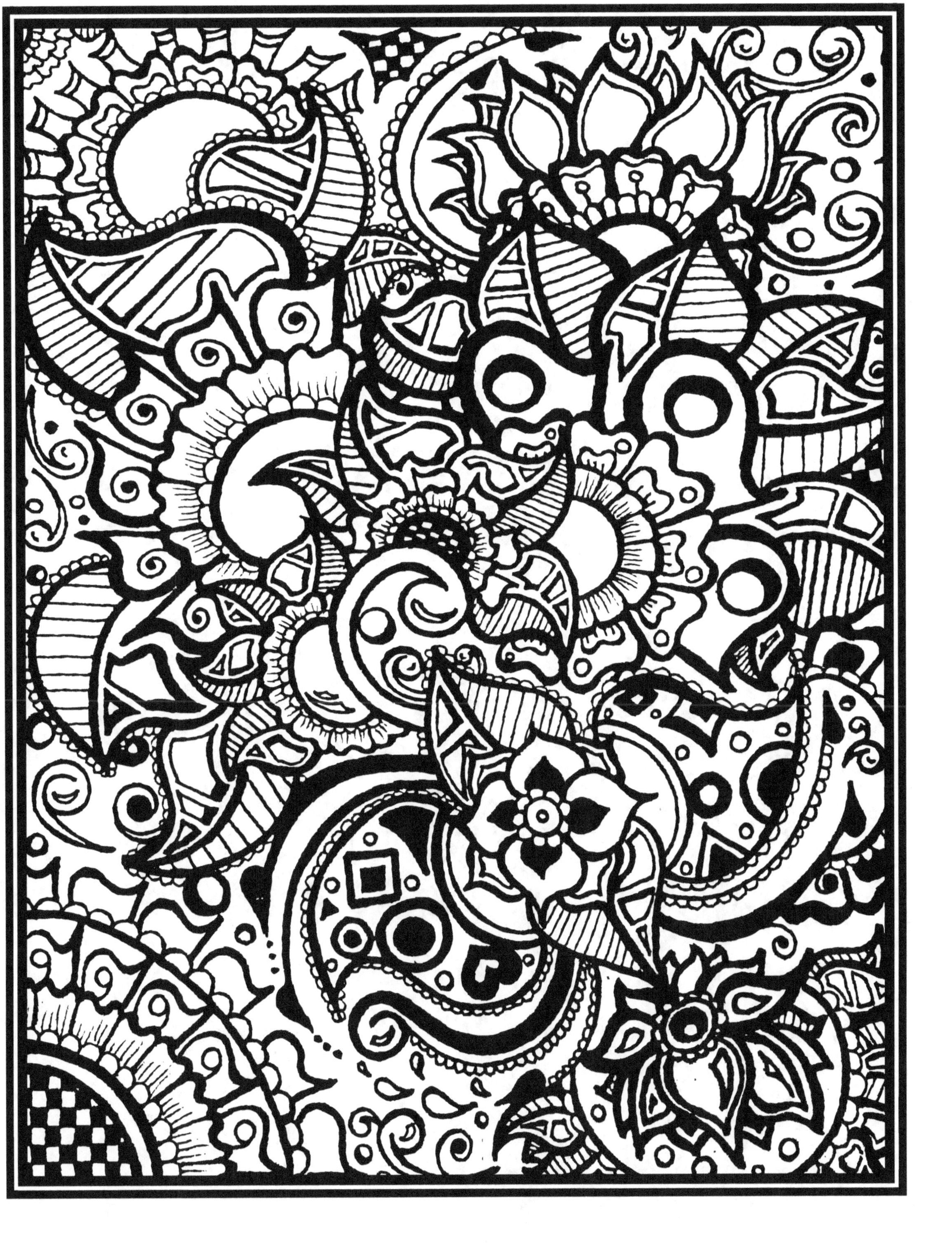

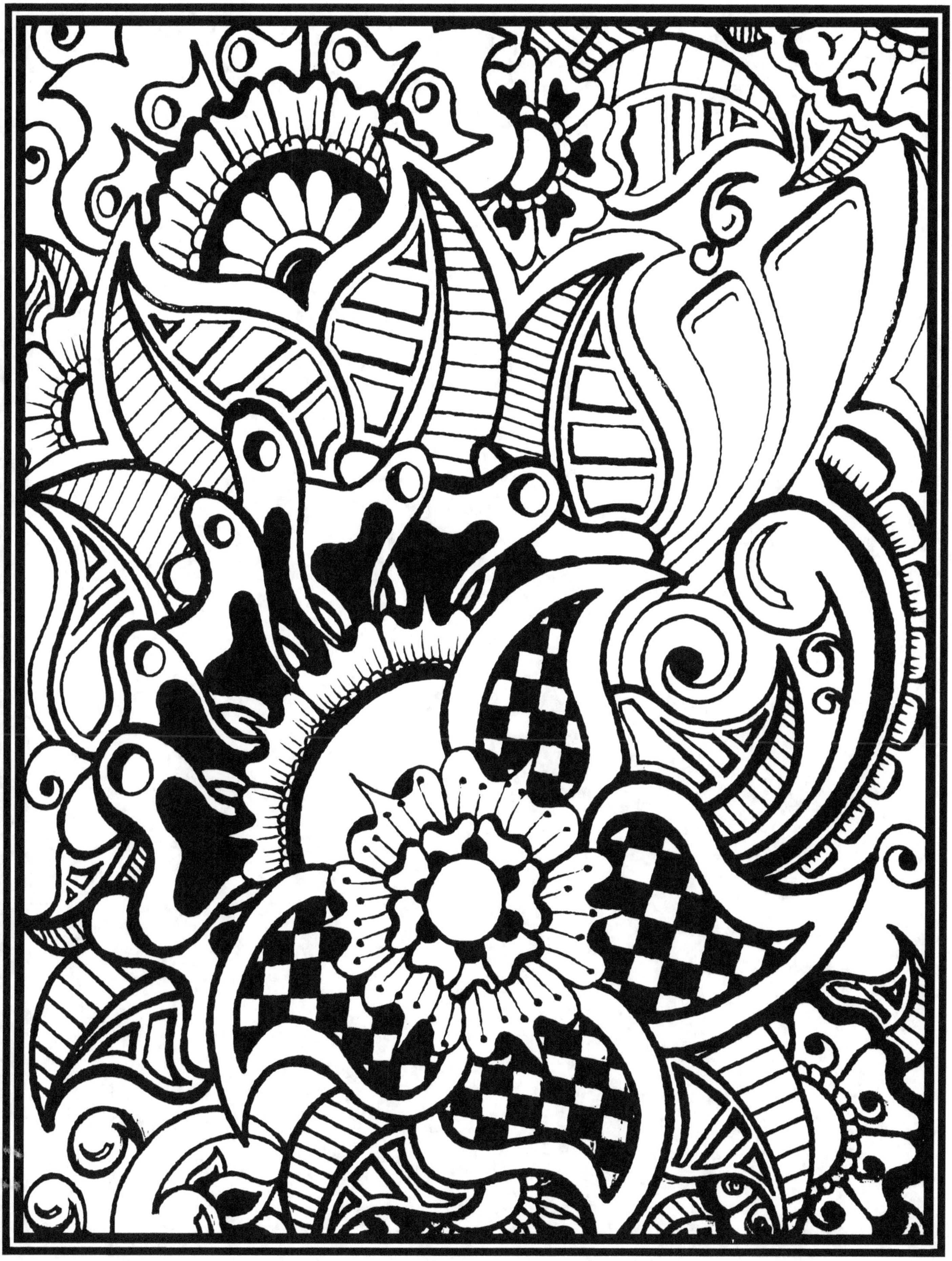

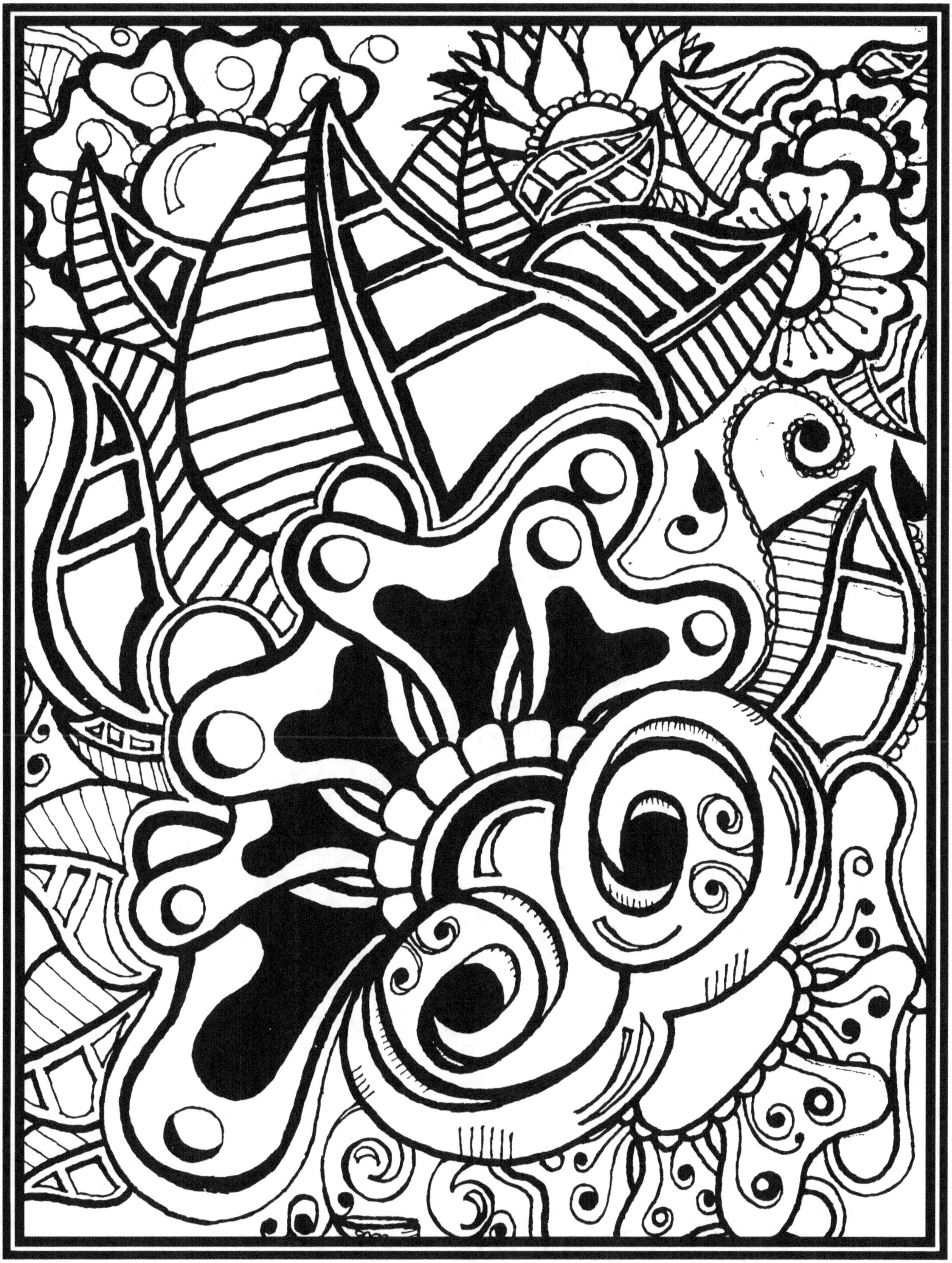

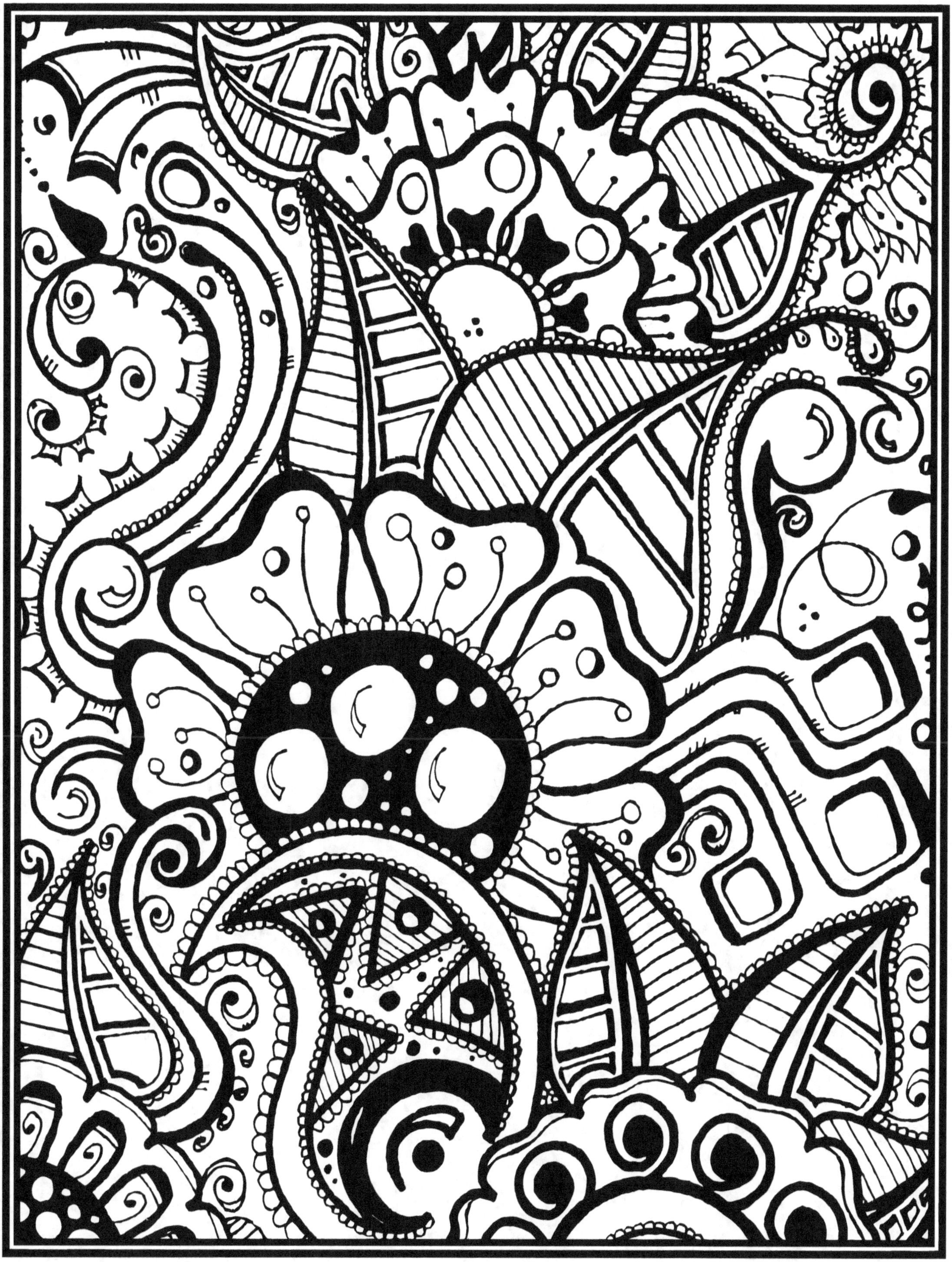

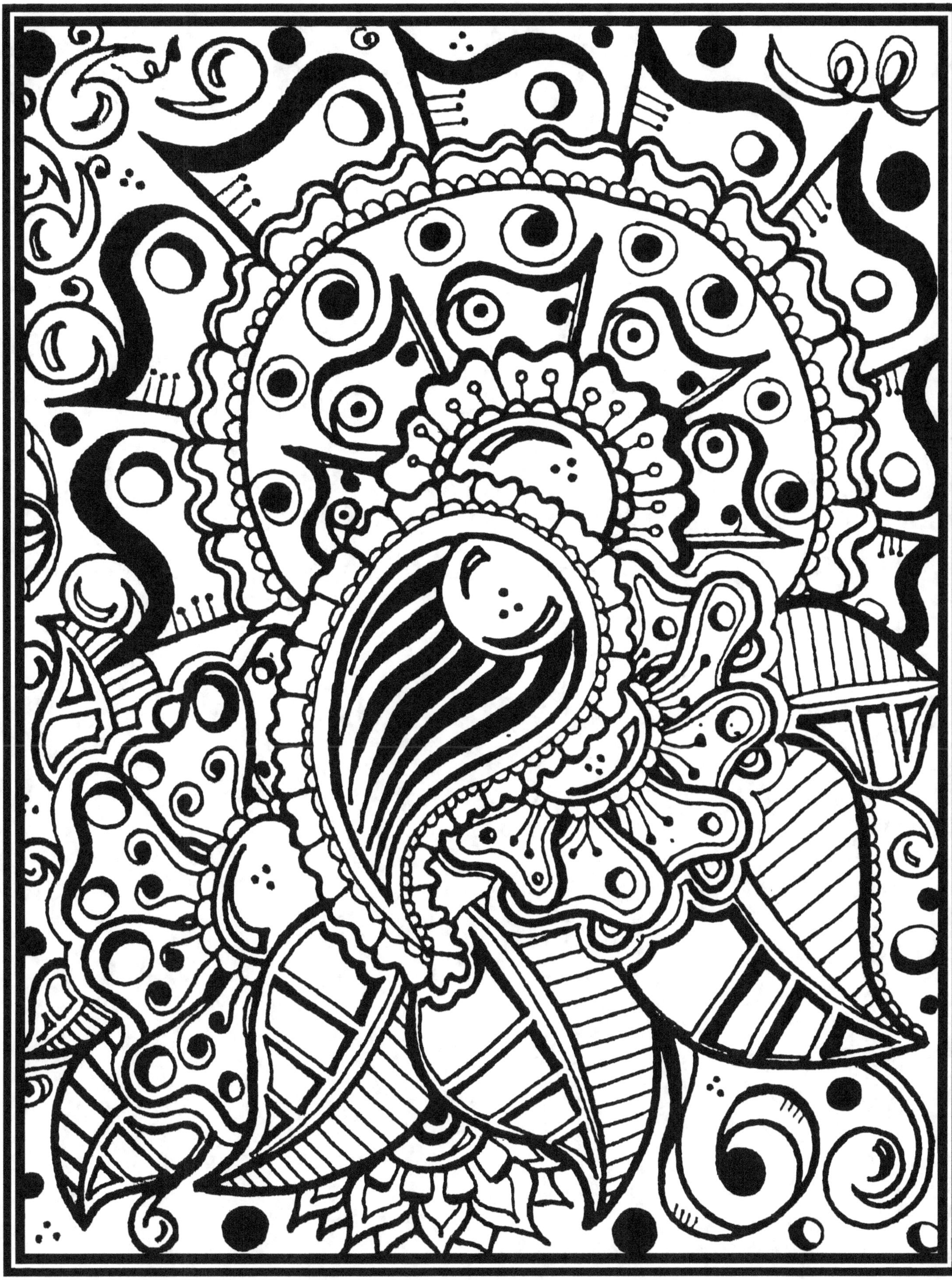

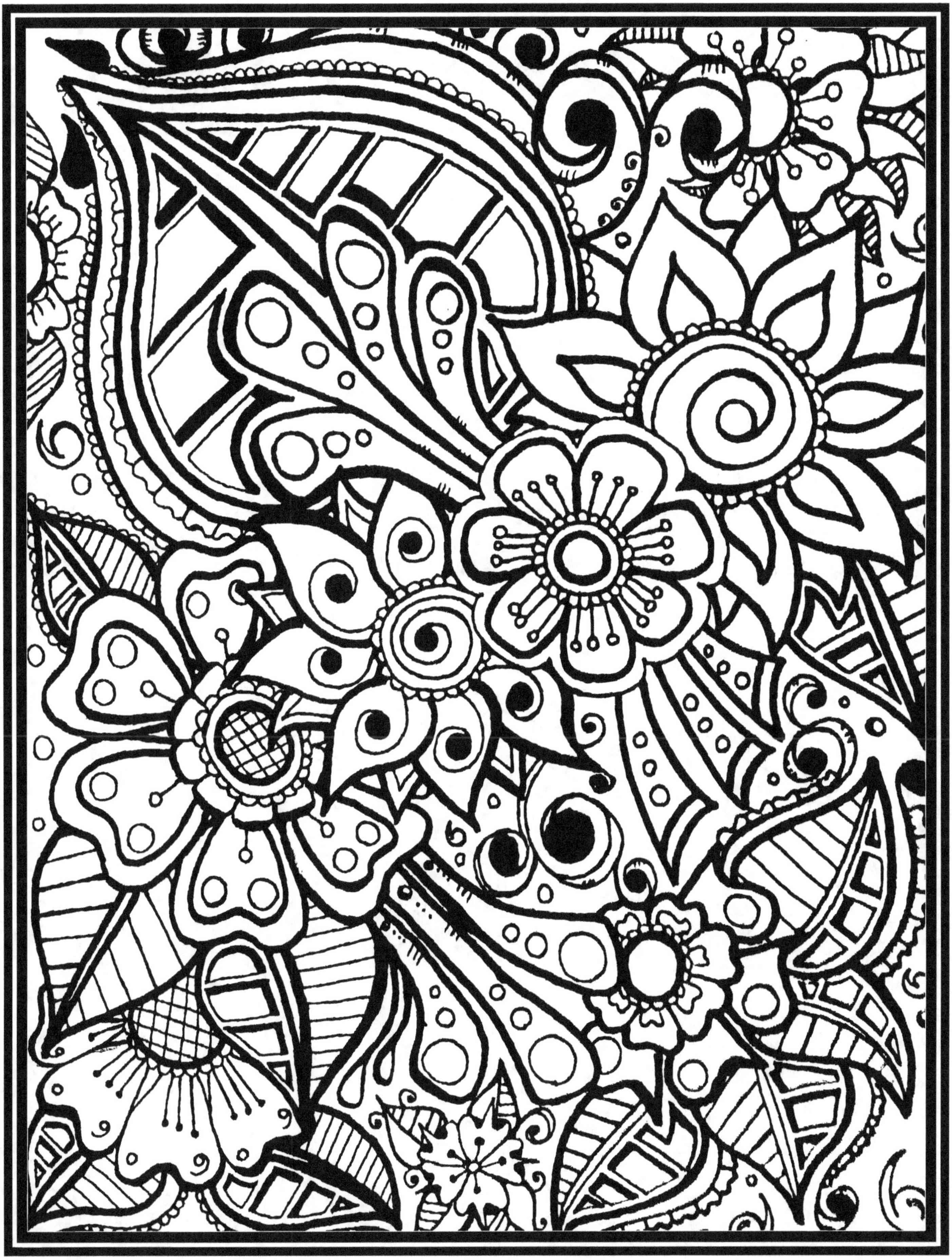

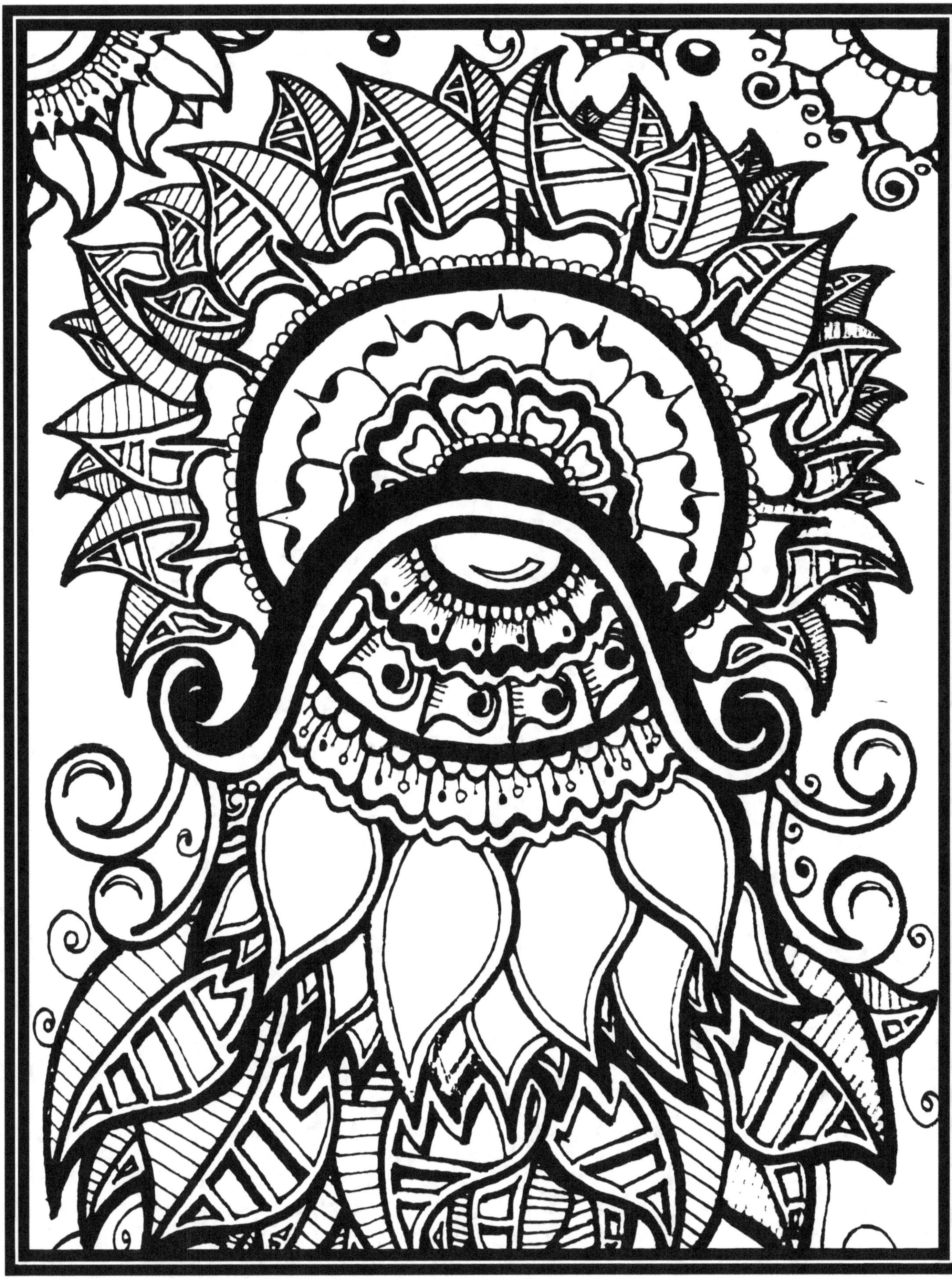

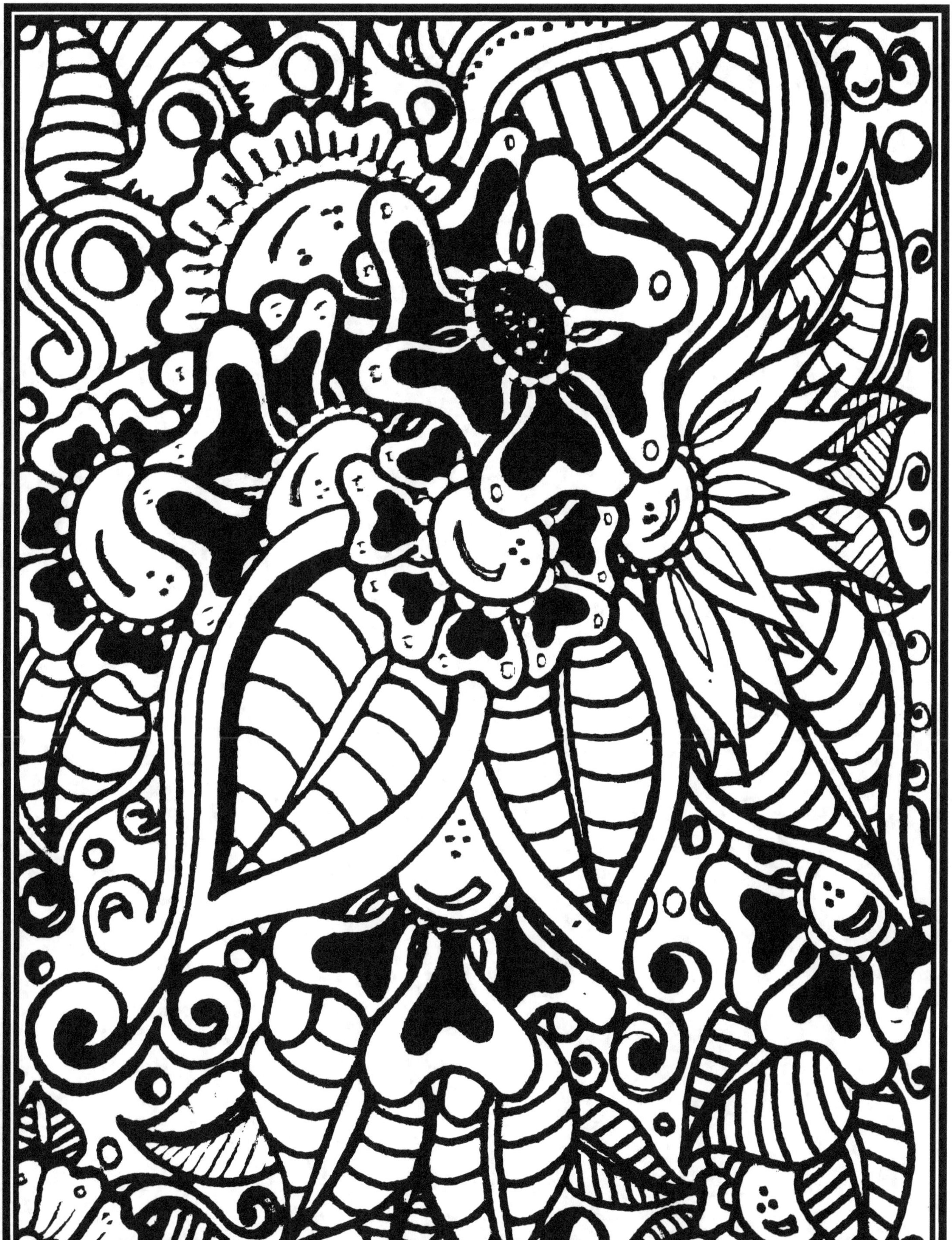

www.ingramcontent.com/pod-product-compliance
Lightning Source LLC
Chambersburg PA
CBHW081434310526
45788CB00023B/3098
* 9 7 8 1 5 4 3 0 6 6 6 9 2 *

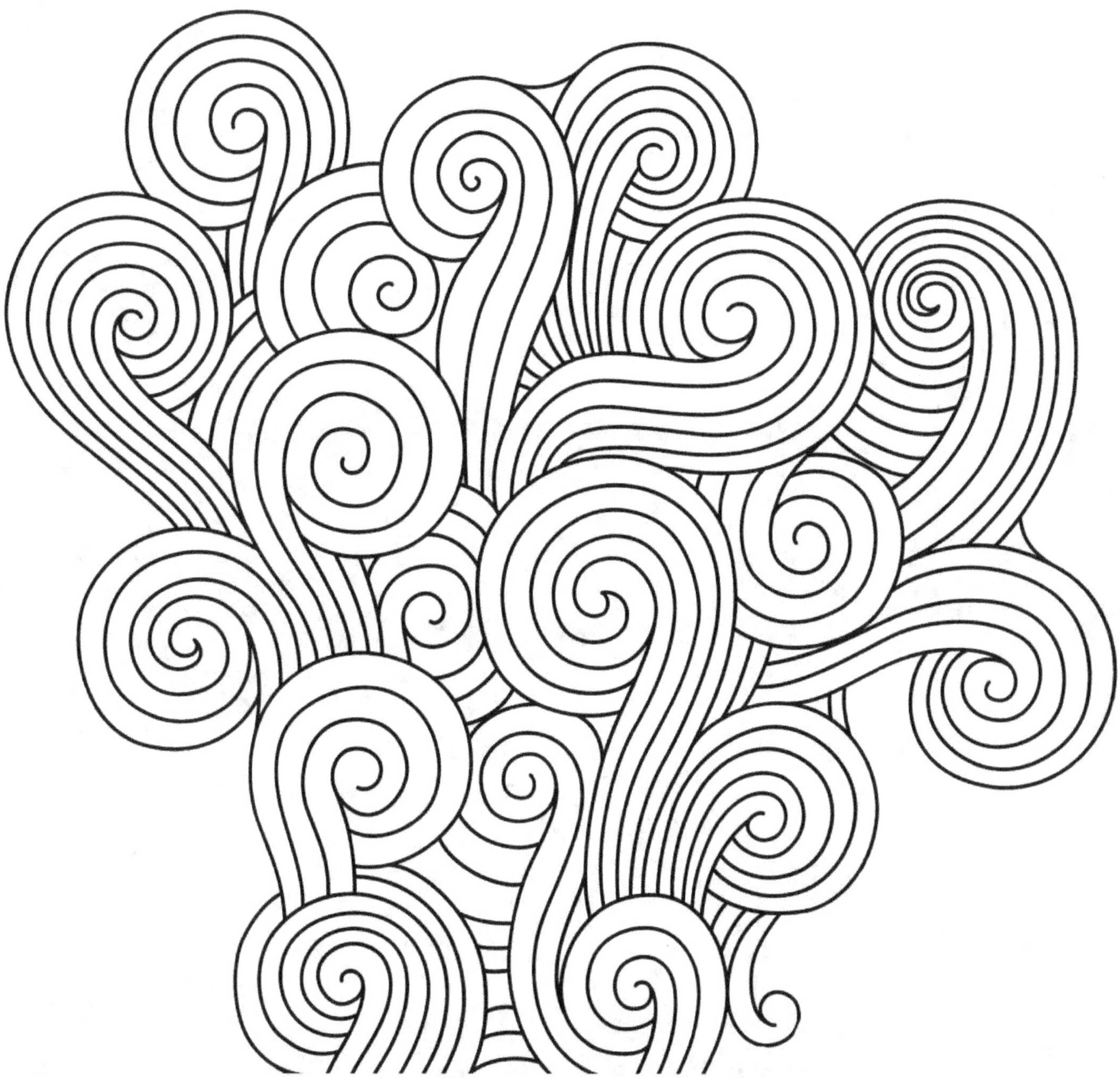

STRESS RELIEVING PATTERNS

EASY FLOWERS

Coloring Book

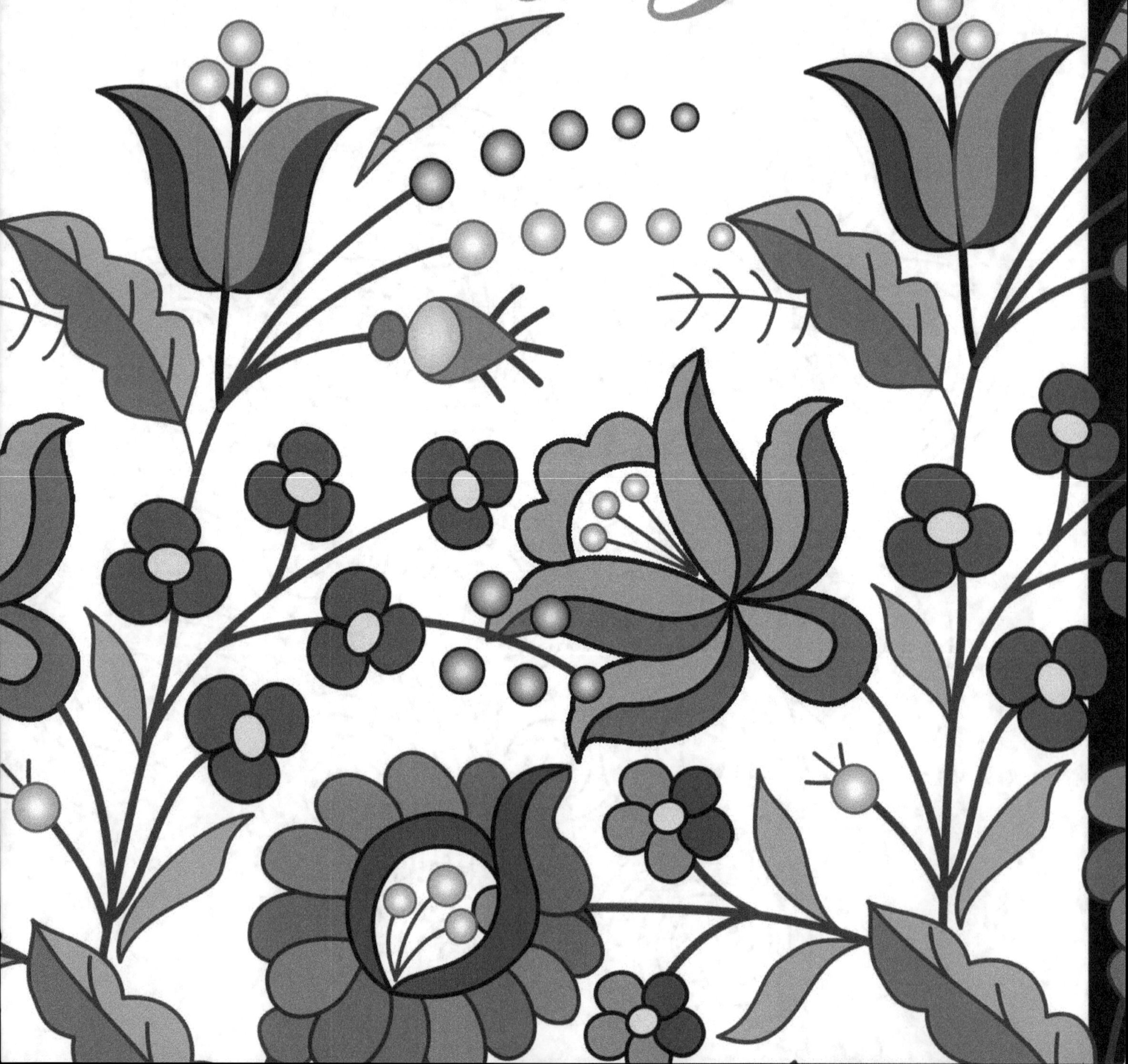